LITERATURE ANTHOLOGIES

# SHORT STORIES

Edited by

**Marjorie Burns and Alice Sherman**

## CURRICULUM CONSULTANTS

*Quality Quinn Sharp, M.A.*
Language Arts Curriculum Specialist
San Marcos Unified School District
San Marcos, California

*Mary C. Glover*
English/Language Arts Consultant
Juvenile Court and Community
 Schools
10083 Canyonside Court
Spring Valley, California

## STAFF

**Editorial Director:**          Edward C. Haggerty
**Art Director:**                Marijka Kostiw
**Editorial Assistant:**         Lisa Crawley

Design of Scholastic Literature Anthologies based on concept by Joe Borzetta.

COVER ILLUSTRATION: Photograph by Peter Mauss of "Arcade, Peck Slip," a trompe l'oeil mural designed by Richard Haas and painted by Seaboard Outdoor Advertising, 1977-78, at the South Street Seaport, New York City. An architect known for his urban murals that juxtapose illusion with reality, Haas designs works that make the viewer step back, look again, and then question where reality ends and illusion begins. Notice that the mural of a seemingly real Brooklyn Bridge is viewed through an imaginary arcade, while in the photograph, towering above in the background is the real Brooklyn Bridge.

### ACKNOWLEDGMENTS

Grateful acknowledgment is made to the following authors and publishers for the use of copyrighted materials. Every effort has been made to obtain permission to use previously published material. Any errors or omissions are unintentional.

**The Attorneys for the Estate of Carson McCullers** for "Sucker" by Carson McCullers. Copyright © 1963 by Carson McCullers. Reprinted by permission of The Attorneys for the Estate of Carson McCullers.
**Toni Cade Bambara** for "My Delicate Heart Condition." Copyright © 1965 by Toni Cade Bambara. Reprinted by permission of the author.
**Gwendolyn Brooks** for "Maud Martha Spares the Mouse" by Gwendolyn Brooks, from MAUD MARTHA. Copyright © 1953 by Gwendolyn Brooks Blakely; "BLACKS," by Gwendolyn Brooks, Copyright © 1987, The DAVID COMPANY, CHICAGO.

*Acknowledgments continued on page 192.*

ISBN 0-590-35440-X

Copyright © 1990 by Scholastic Inc. All rights reserved. Published by Scholastic Inc.

12 11 10 9 8 7 6 5 4 3 2 1          8          9/8 0 1 2 3/9

# CONTENTS

# INTRODUCTION

Every story has two levels of meaning: the *What?* level, and the *So What?* level.

The *What?* level is the story's surface meaning: what happens, when and where it happens, and to whom.

The *So What?* level, which lies beneath the surface, is where you will find the point or purpose of the story. If you could ask the

author about the *So What?* level of a story, you might get an answer like this: "My purpose was to entertain you." Or: "The point is that hypocrisy can do a lot of damage."

To achieve a particular purpose, an author may focus on one of the three basic elements of a story: plot, setting, and character. Of course, every story contains all three elements, but usually the author relies primarily on one element to create an effect or make a point. To help you see the focus each author has chosen, the stories in this book are arranged in three groups, under the headings *plot, setting,* and *character.*

# PART I

# PLOT

The scene on the opposite page looks familiar because it has already been shown on pages 4-5. However, the scene also looks different because it's only one part of the whole picture. Notice that the close-up shows a set of significant details: the goose and the dog looking at the food; the tiger eyeing the other two animals; the safari hunter watching the tiger.

The plot of a short story is also a set of significant details, arranged in a particular pattern. The details in the picture, for example, could be the basis of a story.

The typical short story plot has four parts. The author may start by revealing the situation in which the characters find themselves and the problem or conflict they face. Or, the author may choose to start the action immediately and let information about the characters and their problem emerge gradually.

The author keeps the action moving by reporting the events and actions that grow out of the problem or conflict. If the problem or conflict was not fully revealed at the beginning of the story, you have to discover it for yourself by watching what the characters do and say. Try to identify the opposing forces. They may be a character and the problem he or she is trying to overcome; a character and some external force, such as the sea or a hurricane; or two characters struggling against each other.

The action builds until there is a turning point in the conflict, and one of the opposing forces has to give way. This is the climax of the story, where one force wins and the other loses. The main character defeats the enemy or is defeated; he or she solves the problem or fails to solve it.

Finally, the author shows the results of whatever was decided or revealed at the climax. The plot is resolved, and action stops. The story ends, leaving the characters locked in their final positions forever.

● "A Curious Romance," by Mark Twain, has the simplest possible type of plot: a series of events following one after the other in time. The story has to have this type of plot because it summarizes the factual events in the life of a real person — Dr. James Barry. By the way, the word "romance" in the title doesn't mean that this is a love story. Twain uses the word in its original literary sense, to mean a tale of strange adventures in a far-off, exotic place. In this case, the far-off place is South Africa in the mid-1800's.

# Mark Twain

# A CURIOUS ROMANCE

I SAW SOME OF THE FINE OLD DUTCH MANSIONS, pleasant homes of the early times, pleasant homes today, and enjoyed the privilege of their hospitalities. And just before I sailed I saw in one of them a quaint old picture which was a link in a curious romance — a picture of a pale, intellectual young man in a pink coat with a high black collar. It was a portrait of Dr. James Barry, a military surgeon who came out to the Cape fifty years ago with his regiment. He was a wild young fellow, and was guilty of various kinds of misbehavior. He was several times reported to headquarters in England, and it was in each case expected that orders would come out to deal with him promptly and severely, but for some mysterious reason no orders of any kind came back.

Next, he was promoted — away up. He was made Medical Superintendent-General, and transferred to India. Presently he was back at the Cape again and at his escapades[1] once more. There were plenty of pretty girls, but none of them caught him; evidently he was not a marrying man. And that was another marvel, another puzzle, and made no end of perplexing talk.

Once he was called in the night, on obstetric[2] service, to do what he could for a woman who was believed to be dying. He was prompt and scientific, and saved both mother and child. There are other instances of record which testify to his mastership of his profession. Among other adventures of his was a duel of a desper-

ate sort, fought with swords, at the Castle. He killed his man.

The child heretofore mentioned as having been saved by Dr. Barry so long ago, was named for him and still lives in Cape Town. He had Dr. Barry's portrait painted, and gave it to the gentleman in whose Dutch house I saw it — the quaint figure in the pink coat and high black collar.

The story seems to be arriving nowhere. But that is because I have not finished.

Dr. James Barry died in Cape Town thirty years ago. It was then discovered that he was a *woman*.

[1] **escapades:** reckless adventures
[2] **obstetric:** a branch of medicine dealing with childbirth

## A CLOSER LOOK

*1. What effect does Twain achieve in this story? Or, to ask the question in another way, what was your reaction to the story?*

*2. Twain realizes that without the surprise ending, this story would not be worth telling. In which sentence does he say that he realizes this?*

● There's nothing unusual about praying to God. But writing a letter to God is an entirely different story!

# Gregorio Lopez y Fuentes

# A LETTER TO GOD

*Translated by Donald A. Yates*

THE HOUSE — THE ONLY ONE IN THE ENTIRE valley — sat on the crest[1] of a low hill. From this height one could see the river and, next to the corral,[2] the field of ripe corn dotted with the kidney bean flowers that always promised a good harvest.

The only thing the earth needed was a rainfall, or at least a shower. Throughout the morning Lencho — who knew his fields intimately — had done nothing else but scan the sky toward the northeast.

"Now we're really going to get some water, woman."

The woman, who was preparing supper, replied: "Yes, God willing."

The oldest boys were working in the field, while the smaller ones were playing near the house, until the woman called to them all: "Come for dinner. . . ."

It was during the meal that, just as Lencho had predicted, big drops of rain began to fall. In the northeast huge mountains of clouds could be seen approaching. The air was fresh and sweet.

The man went out to look for something in the corral for no other reason than to allow himself the pleasure of feeling the rain on his body, and when he returned he exclaimed: "Those aren't raindrops falling from the sky, they're new coins. The big drops are ten-centavo[3] pieces and the little ones are fives. . . ."

With a satisfied expression he regarded the field of ripe corn with its kidney bean flowers, draped in a curtain of rain. But suddenly a strong wind began to blow and, together with the rain, very large hailstones began to fall. These truly did resemble new silver coins. The boys, exposing themselves to the rain, ran out to collect the frozen pearls.

"It's really geting bad now," exclaimed the man, mortified. "I hope it passes quickly."

It did not pass quickly. For an hour the hail rained on the house, the garden, the hillside, the cornfield, on the whole valley. The field was white, as if covered with salt. Not a leaf remained on the trees. The corn was totally destroyed. The flowers were gone from the kidney bean plants. Lencho's soul was filled with sadness. When the storm had passed, he stood in the middle of the field and said to his sons: "A plague of locusts would have left more than this. . . . The hail has left nothing: this year we will have no corn or beans. . . ."

That night was a sorrowful one: "All our work, for nothing!"

"There's no one who can help us!"

"We'll all go hungry this year. . . ."

But in the hearts of all who lived in that solitary house in the middle of the valley, there was a single hope: help from God.

"Don't be so upset, even though this seems like a total loss. Remember, no one dies of hunger!"

"That's what they say: no one dies of hunger. . . ."

All through the night, Lencho thought only of his one hope: the help of God, whose eyes, as he had been instructed, see everything, even what is deep in one's conscience.

Lencho was an ox of a man, working like an animal in the fields, but still he knew how to write. The following Sunday, at daybreak, after having convinced himself that there is a protecting spirit, he began to write a letter which he himself would carry to town and place in the mail.

It was nothing less than a letter to God.

"God," he wrote, "if you don't help me, my family and I will go hungry this year. I need a hundred pesos[4] in order to resow the field and to live until the crop comes, because the hailstorm . . ."

He wrote "To God" on the envelope, put the letter inside and, still troubled, went to town. At the post office he placed a stamp on the letter and dropped it into the mailbox.

One of the employees, who was a postman and also helped at the post office, went to his boss, laughing heartily, and showed him the letter to God. Never in his career as a postman had he known that address. The postmaster — a fat, amiable[5] fellow — also broke out laughing, but almost immediately he turned serious and, tapping the letter on his desk, commented: "What faith! I wish I had the faith of the man who wrote this letter. To believe the way

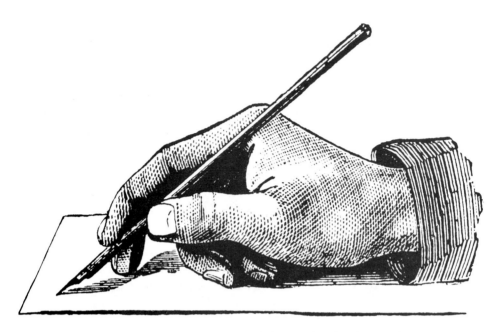

he believes. To hope with the confidence that he knows how to hope with. Starting up a correspondence with God!"

So, in order not to disillusion that prodigy[6] of faith, revealed by a letter that could not be delivered, the postmaster came up with an idea: answer the letter. But when he opened it, it was evident that to answer it he needed something more than good will, ink and paper. But he stuck to his resolution: he asked for money from his employee, he himself gave part of his salary, and several friends of his were obliged to give something "for an act of charity."

It was impossible for him to gather together the hundred *pesos* requested by Lencho, so he was able to send the farmer only a little more than half. He put the bills in an envelope addressed to Lencho and with them a letter containing only a signature:

GOD

The following Sunday Lencho came a bit earlier than usual to ask if there was a letter for him. It was the postman himself who handed the letter to him, while the postmaster, experiencing the contentment of a man who has performed a good deed, looked on from the doorway of his office.

Lencho showed not the slightest surprise on seeing the bills — such was his confidence — but he became angry when he counted the money. God could not have made a mistake, nor could he have denied Lencho what he had requested!

Immediately, Lencho went up to the window to ask for paper and ink. On the public writing table, he started to write, with much wrinkling of his brow, caused by the effort he had to make to express his ideas. When he finished, he went to the window to buy a stamp, which he licked and then affixed to the envelope with a blow of his fist.

The moment that the letter fell into the mailbox the postmaster went to open it. It said:

"God: Of the money that I asked for, only seventy pesos reached me. Send me the rest, since I need it very much. But don't send it to me through the mail, because the post office employees are a bunch of crooks. Lencho."

[1] **crest:** top of a hill
[2] **corral:** an enclosure for livestock
[3] **centavo:** coin used in many Latin-American countries
[4] **peso:** 100 centavos make a peso
[5] **amiable:** friendly; agreeable
[6] **prodigy:** something extraordinary; a marvel

## A CLOSER LOOK

*1. The letter to God leads the postmaster to a conclusion about Lencho's feelings toward God. What is that conclusion? In your answer, explain what Lencho has that the postmaster wishes he had too.*

*2. Why does the postmaster want to give Lencho the money he asked God to send him? Put yourself in the postmaster's place. What would you say to your friends to persuade them to contribute?*

*3. When he sees the bills enclosed with the letter from "God," Lencho shows no surprise. Why not? After counting the bills, Lencho writes another letter, asking God for the rest of the money. But this time he tells God not to send the money through the mail. Explain why.*

*4. A situation is **ironic** when it turns out to be the opposite of what is expected. Explain why the ending of "A Letter to God" is ironic. In your answer, contrast what you expected to happen at the end with what actually did happen.*

● The dog knew how to herd cattle. It wanted to be needed, and it longed for affection. It could have been useful to the old man and his nephew in this part of Australia. But the old man insisted it was "good for nothin'."

## Alan Marshall

# THE DOG

THE DOG DROPPED TO ITS HAUNCHES AND scratched itself vigorously behind the ear with its hind foot.

"That there dog's lousy,"[1] said the old man. "I always told you it were lousy." But his nephew was asleep.

Having relieved the itch, the dog turned and surveyed the old man with a calm, contemplative look as if pondering on the reasons for the enmity[2] of this gentle, white-haired old pipe-sucker.

The dog had been a stray dog. This was a handicap. For stray dogs are looked on with suspicion by those with whom they would be friendly. A fortnight[3] ago it had followed a swagman[4] for many miles, occasionally wagging its tail as a sign of its desire to be companionable. But the tramp disliked dogs, and at their first stopping place had kicked the animal. This discourtesy offended the dog and it had left him.

It followed a side track and came upon a young man walking behind a heifer[5] that constantly sought to break back and return to the paddock[6] whence it was being taken.

The dog's great-grandfather had lived with a drover.[7] The dog barked furiously and dashed at that homesick cow with an obvious determination. The heifer, after a wild dash through brushing gumsuckers, decided to go quietly. It knew a good dog when it felt one.

The dog approached the young man, wagging its tail and panting in a friendly fashion. It felt confident that it had done well.

The young man took a pipe from his pocket and began to fill it. He surveyed the dog with an amused, tolerant smile upon his brown face, as if he were thinking, "You old character."

The dog interpreted this as being favorable to the possibility of an immediate adoption. It commenced[8] showing off by dashing round in small circles, its tail held hard down. It barked and whisked around while the young man watched it in his amused and interested way.

He struck a match to light his pipe and, while sucking the flame into the dark, seasoned bowl, kept his eyes turned on the dog. His pipe alight, he flicked the burnt match-end to the road and blew a mushroom of smoke into the air.

"Good boy," he said, and commenced to walk after the cow.

The dog followed him.

That had been a fortnight ago.

The dog had made a mistake and scratched itself when being introduced to the old man. But it had never regarded scratching as being objectionable. All the dogs it knew scratched themselves. Fleas were part of dogs like the old man's pipe was of him. So the dog continued scratching itself, being loath to forgo the pleasure merely to please so narrow-minded a person.

The dog looked very thoughtful as it lay and watched the old man.

"Get out," said the old man.

The dog ignored this. It thumped the floor with its tail and tried to convey by the expression in its soft brown eyes its desire to be friendly.

The nephew sat up. He stretched his arms above his head and yawned.

"Growling at the dog, Unc?" he asked cheerfully. "He's all right, aren't you Spot?"

The dog approached the nephew. Its hindquarters wobbled from side to side with the energy it put into the wagging of its tail. It wore a humble and devoted look.

"That there dog is good for nothin'," said the old man.

He had a quiet, gentle voice. One instantly knew him to be a good man. Upon his feet he wore those soft, black leather boots known as "Romeos." They were fastened with a buckle catch.

"I like dogs, but not lousy dogs."

"I don't like anything that's lousy," said the nephew. "Give me a look at you, Spot."

He parted the hair on the dog's back, looking for fleas.

"Not a sign of one, Unc. All dogs scratch themselves."

"I got fleas offen him," persisted the old man, "I never felt no fleas until he come."

"Hm!" said the nephew.

The old man's dislike became a serious problem to the dog. I imagine that it at last determined to rid itself of the fleas it nourished.

In a small clearing to the left of the house, a cow had died. White ribs like rafters showed through breaks in the dry skin. The interior was hollow. The thin tail of a goanna[9] could often be seen protruding through a hole in the carcass while its owner picked at the dried shreds of flesh that still adhered to the bones.

Around the carcass, the grass had withered and died, making a discolored border where decaying flesh had returned to the soil.

One sunny morning the dog visited this spot. It was full of business. Over and over in that foul border it rolled. It rubbed its head, its neck, its body among the dead, corrupt grass. It shook itself and rolled again.

At last, confident in the success of its scheme, it returned joyfully to the house where the old man and his nephew were eating their breakfast.

Its entrance made the old man stay proceeding on[10] his fried chop.

"That there dog stinks," he said with prompt conviction.

The nephew laid down his knife and sniffed the air.

"I can't smell anything, Unc."

"Cripes!" exclaimed the old man, his face twisted in distaste.

A breeze floating through the doorway passed over the dog on its way to stir the curly, tousled hair on the nephew's head.

He jumped violently up from his chair.

"Phew!"

The dog retired hurriedly through the open door. It had offended the nephew. Terrible.

It made for the dam where it squatted in the yellow water, lapping at it with its pink tongue. Later it dried itself in the sun on the clay bank.

Shadows of swallows moved across and around it and out over the water. It wondered whether the smell had gone. It rose and visited the old man.

He eyed it suspiciously, but though he sniffed with evident anticipation he found nothing to take exception to. It was an anxious moment for the dog.

In the far corner of the house paddock[11] near the bank of a dried

watercourse was an old mining shaft. Gold had been found there. The windlass[12] that had once creaked to the slow winding of bowyanged[13] miners now slept in the quiet sunshine. Kookaburras[14] flew to it from the grass. They scraped their bills against its bleached wood and sat there, head on one side, watching the ground for movements of live things.

On the brink of the shaft, between it and one of the fences, a twisted yellow box tree had grown. One limb hung over the gaping mouth. The roots found nourishment in the round mound of clay and stone that had been raised from below.

In the small triangle of space made by the shaft and the meeting fences the nephew had planted a willow cutting. In such a spot it was safe from cattle and horses. Occasionally, he visited it and the old windlass would creak once more to a laden bucket as he raised water to refresh its drooping leaves.

To reach the cutting, the nephew would grasp the limb of the yellow box and lean out over the shaft as he stepped round the tree on to the plot that harbored the little willow.

Sometimes, with his hand tightly grasping the limb, he would look down and there, below, he could see the cold gleam of dark water.

The dog usually accompanied him. It watched the raising of the bucket with interest. The nephew would sometimes let him drink from it.

On one of these visits a rabbit occupied the attention of the dog for a few minutes. When it returned the nephew had disappeared. A broken branch of the yellow box tree lay across the shaft's mouth.

The dog was interested. It ran forward and looked down the shaft with its ears pricked, its tail wagging. The sound of splashing came from below. It could see the nephew's white, round face moving in the darkness.

The dog became very excited. It padded with its feet on the brink, barking and enjoying itself.

From the water, whose black surface wavered with reflected gleams, the nephew spoke to the dog.

"Go home, boy. Good boy. G'way back."

But the dog did not understand.

It barked and ran to and fro on the edge of the shaft. The nephew urged it, implored it. Suddenly the dog became afraid. It whined and peered into the darkness. It was very still down there. It heard the nephew's voice, speaking as if to himself:

"Damn the dog."

He spoke with feeling. The tone was derogatory[15] and hopeless.

The dog ran a little way from the shaft, then stopped and looked back. It whined to itself and fidgeted on its feet. It took a few steps towards the shaft, but suddenly, as if realizing the desperate plight of its friend, it turned and raced towards the house.

How beautifully it ran. Its long hair floated along with it. Its tongue swung from the side of its mouth.

It bounded into the kitchen where the old man was peering into a saucepan on the stove and poking gently at the contents with a fork.

The old man got quite a fright. An involuntary "That there dog" came from his lips.

The dog made a stand in front of him, barking loudly. This behavior astounded the old man. With the fork poised in the air he regarded the dog as if it were a strange dog, a formidable dog.

The dog suddenly rushed forward and seized the old man's trousers. It pulled back violently. The old man almost lost his balance. He flung out his arms and staggered. He put a table between him and the dog.

The dog's bark took on a whining note. It ran to the door and stopped, looked back at the old man.

The old man's expression suddenly changed. His face became white. He hurried from behind the table. The dog bounded ahead.

The old man followed. The wind stirred the white, silken hair on his head. Then he realized where the dog was leading him and he commenced running. What was almost a moan came from his lips and he ran as he had never run before.

His face, usually so placid, was strained; his eyes were wide and fixed. But he was old and his joints were stiff. His fastest speed was slow to the dog.

It reached the shaft ahead of him and stood on the brink barking, looking first into the darkness and then towards the old man as if he wished to convey to the nephew the assurance that help was coming.

The old man kept running. Not far now, but his poor legs had weakened and his heart beat painfully. He stumbled on the loose stones that lay along the track. He was breathless when he reached the foot of the yellow box tree.

He dreaded a silence from the cold, horrible well, but his nephew's voice came to him, weak, a little muffled.

"Hurry, Unc."

He hurried, almost hindering himself with his fumbling hands. The bucket rattled down the gaping hole until a splash and a slackened rope showed that it had reached the water.

"Wind slowly, Unc. The rope is rotten."

He commenced to wind. Very slowly. His eyes were closed, his lips parted a little. His throat was twitching. How old he was. Ah! age was cruel! Once his knees almost gave and the winding stopped, but he instantly recovered and went on again.

At last the nephew's dripping head appeared. He grasped the windlass and with an effort hoisted himself onto solid ground. He lay there a moment exhausted.

His task done, the old man became strangely weak. He leant on the windlass handle feeling ill. The nephew staggered to his feet and went to him. He lifted him and laid him on the ground.

"Are you all right, Unc?" he asked anxiously.

He squeezed water from his coat onto the face of the old man. The old man shook his head and sat up. He felt for his pipe and, finding it, discovered that his shaking hands could not light it. His nephew took the matches and, striking one, held the cupped flame to the bowl. He smiled into the face of the old man and said:

"Good for you, Unc."

The dog thought the time opportune to express relief at the nephew's escape. It wished to lick his hand. It advanced in a conciliatory[16] way with an eye on the old man whose wrath[17] it regarded as certain. Its eyes almost pleaded with him.

The old man took his pipe from his mouth and looked long and earnestly at the dog.

"That there dog's a good dog," he said.

[1] **lousy:** full of lice; but when the uncle uses the word, he means "full of fleas"
[2] **enmity:** hatred
[3] **fortnight:** 14 days
[4] **swagman:** wanderer without a permanent home; vagrant
[5] **heifer:** a young cow
[6] **paddock:** an enclosed area
[7] **drover:** a person who drives cattle or sheep
[8] **commenced:** began
[9] **goanna:** large lizard
[10] **stay proceedings on:** stop eating
[11] **house paddock:** fenced-in yard
[12] **windlass:** machine for winding and unwinding a rope
[13] **bowyang:** strap used to hitch up trousers under the knee
[14] **Kookaburras:** birds about the size of crows
[15] **derogatory:** unfavorable, belittling
[16] **conciliatory:** tending to win over or make peaceful
[17] **wrath:** anger

## A CLOSER LOOK

*1. The dog in this story understands and reacts to what is being said. Find examples in which the dog demonstrates this human quality of comprehension.*

*2. Who is the central character in the story? How do you know? From whose point of view is the story told — the dog's or the humans'?*

*3. Because it cannot speak, the dog runs into problems in communicating with humans. Describe one of those problems. Then tell what the dog does to make itself understood.*

*4. A flashback is a device which interrupts the action of a story to show an episode that happened at an earlier time. In "The Dog," the author starts by telling us that there is a conflict between the old man and the dog. Then, having aroused our curiosity about the conflict, he uses a flashback (paragraphs 4 through 14) to provide background information about the dog's problem. If the author had told us about the dog's background before telling us about the conflict, would he have been as successful in drawing us into the story? Why or why not?*

● "The Diamond Necklace" is the work of a master plot-maker. It was written in 1884 and takes place in Paris, France. But, like all great stories, the subject matter is both timeless and universal. We all know how it feels to long for things we don't have. It's what we do about these longings that determines the quality of our lives.

## Guy de Maupassant

# THE DIAMOND NECKLACE

SHE WAS ONE OF THOSE PRETTY, CHARMING young ladies, born, as if through an error of destiny, into a family of clerks. She had no dowry[1] . . . no hopes for the future . . . no means of becoming known, appreciated, loved, and married by a man either rich or distinguished. And she allowed herself to marry a petty clerk in the office of the Board of Education.

She dressed with tasteful simplicity, not being able to adorn herself, but she was unhappy at being denied her rightful place in society. For women belong to no caste,[2] no class: their grace, beauty, and charm serve them in the place of birth and family. Their inborn finesse,[3] their instinctive elegance, their suppleness of wit are their only aristocracy, making some daughters of the common people the equal of great ladies.

Feeling herself born for all delicacies and luxuries, she suffered incessantly from the poverty of her apartment, the shabby walls, worn chairs, and faded fabrics. All these things, which another woman of her station would not have noticed, tortured and angered her. The sight of the little Breton girl who did the household chores awoke in her sad regrets and desperate dreams. She thought of quiet antechambers[4] with Oriental wall hangings, lighted by high bronze torches, and of the two tall footmen in knee-breeches who would doze in the large armchairs, made sleepy by the heavy air from the heating apparatus. She thought of large drawing rooms hung with old silks, of graceful pieces of furniture holding priceless knick-knacks, and of little perfumed, coquettish boudoirs[5] made for five o'clock chats with most intimate friends — men

21

known and sought after, men whose attention all women envied and desired.

When she seated herself for dinner at the round table where the tablecloth already showed three days' use, and her husband uncovered the tureen with a delighted expression on his face, saying: "Oh! A good potpie! I know nothing better than that!" — she would think of elegant dinners, of shining silver, of tapestries[6] peopling the walls with ancient personages and rare birds in the midst of fairy forests. And she would think of the exquisite food served on marvelous dishes at such dinners, and of whispered gallantries[7] to which she would listen with the smile of a sphinx[8] while she ate the rose-colored flesh of a trout or a chicken's wing.

She had neither gowns nor jewels, nothing. And those were the only things she cared about. She felt that she was meant to have them. She longed so fervently to please, to be clever, to be sought after and courted.

She had a rich friend, a former schoolmate at the convent, whom she did not like to visit because she suffered so much when she came home. She would weep for whole days afterward, from misery, regret, disappointment, and despair.

One evening her husband came home elated, bearing in his hand a large envelope. "Here," said he, "here is something for you."

She quickly tore open the envelope and drew out a printed card on which were inscribed these words:

> "The Minister of Public Instruction and Madame
> George Ramponneau request the honor of Monsieur and
> Madame Loisel's company Monday evening, January
> 18, at the Minister's residence."

Instead of being delighted, as her husband had expected, she threw the invitation spitefully onto the table, murmuring, "What do you suppose I want with that?"

"But, my dear, I thought it would make you happy. You never go out, and this is an occasion, a fine one! I went to a great deal of trouble to get this invitation. Everybody wants one, and not many are given to employees — it is a very exclusive affair. You'll see the whole official world there."

She gave him an irritated look and asked impatiently, "What do you suppose I have to wear to such an occasion?"

He had not thought of that. He stammered, "Why, the dress you wear when we go to the theater. It seems very pretty to me —"

He fell silent, stupefied, at the sight of his wife weeping. Two large tears were rolling slowly from the corners of her eyes toward the corners of her mouth. "What is the matter?" he stammered. "What is the matter?"

With a violent effort she controlled her vexation and, wiping her moist cheeks, responded in a calm voice: "Nothing. Only I have nothing to wear, and consequently I cannot go to this affair. Give your invitation to some colleague whose wife is better fitted out than I."

He was grieved, but answered: "Let's see, Matilda. How much would a suitable dress cost, something that would serve for other occasions, something very simple?"

She reflected for a few seconds, making estimates and trying to think of a sum that she could ask for without getting a frightened exclamation and an immediate refusal from the frugal clerk. Finally she said hesitantly, "I can't tell exactly, but it seems to me that four hundred francs[9] ought to cover it."

He turned slightly pale, for he had saved just this sum to buy a gun so that he could join some hunting parties the next summer, on the plains at Nanterre, with some friends who went up there on Sundays to shoot larks. Nevertheless, he answered, "Very well. I will give you four hundred francs. But try to get a pretty dress."

The day of the ball approached and Mme. Loisel seemed sad, disturbed, anxious, although her dress was nearly ready. One evening her husband said to her, "What's the matter with you? You've been acting strangely for the last two or three days."

She answered, "I'm annoyed that I don't have even one piece of jewelry to adorn myself with. I shall look so poverty-stricken! I would rather not go to the party."

"You can wear some fresh flowers," he replied. "At this season they look very chic. For ten francs you can have two or three magnificent roses."

She was not convinced. "No," she answered, "there is nothing more humiliating than to have a shabby look in the midst of rich women."

Then her husband cried out: "How stupid we are! Go and find your friend Mme. Forestier and ask her to lend you some of her jewels. You know her well enough to do that."

She uttered a cry of joy. "That's true! I never thought of that!"

The next day she went to her friend's house and related her tale of distress. Mme. Forestier went to her closet with the mirrored doors, took out a large jewel case, brought it, opened it, and said, "Choose, my dear."

First she saw some bracelets, then a collar of pearls, then a Venetian cross of very fine workmanship, made of gold and precious stones. She tried on each piece before the mirror, but could not decide what she wanted. "Have you nothing else?" she asked.

"Why, yes. Look for yourself. I can't tell what you'll like."

Suddenly she discovered, in a black satin box, a superb necklace of diamonds, and her heart beat fast with an immoderate desire. Her hands trembled as she took them up. She placed them about her throat against her dress, and stood looking at herself in ecstasy. Then she asked hesitantly, in a voice full of anxiety, "Could you lend me this? Just this?"

"Why, yes, certainly."

She threw her arms around her friend's neck, then went away with her treasure.

The day of the ball arrived. Mme. Loisel was a great success. She was the prettiest of all — elegant, gracious, smiling, and full of joy. All the men noticed her, asked her name, and wanted to be introduced. All the members of the Cabinet wanted to waltz with her. The Minister of Education paid her some attention.

She danced enthusiastically, passionately, intoxicated with plea-sure and thinking of nothing in the triumph of her beauty, the glory of her success, moving in a kind of cloud of happiness that came of all this homage, this admiration, these awakened desires, this victory so complete and sweet to the heart of woman.

She went home at about four o'clock in the morning. Her hus-band had been half asleep in one of the little salons[10] since mid-night, with three other men whose wives were enjoying themselves very much.

He threw around her shoulders one of the wraps they had

brought to wear home, a modest everyday garment whose poverty clashed with the elegance of the ball costume. She felt this, and wished to hurry away so she would not be noticed by the other women, who were wrapping themselves in rich furs.

Loisel held her back. "Wait," said he. "You'll catch cold out there. I am going to call a cab."

But she would not listen, and descended the steps rapidly. When they got out to the street they found no carriage, and they began to look for one, hailing the coachmen whom they saw at a distance.

They walked along toward the Seine,[11] hopeless and shivering. Finally they found on the dock one of those old coupés[12] that one sees in Paris only after nightfall, as if they were ashamed to show their misery in the daylight.

It took them to their door in Martyr Street, and they went wearily up to their apartment. It was all over for her. As for him, he remembered that he would have to be at the office by ten o'clock.

She removed the wrap from her shoulders before the mirror, for a final view of herself in her glory. Suddenly she uttered a cry. Her necklace was not around her neck.

Her husband, already half undressed, asked, "What's the matter?"

She turned toward him in panic. "I've — I've — I don't have Mme. Forestier's necklace anymore!"

He rose in dismay. "What? How's that? It's impossible!"

And they looked in the folds of the dress, in the folds of the wrap, in the pockets, everywhere. They could not find it.

He asked, "Are you sure you still had it when we left the Minister's house?"

"Yes. I felt it in the vestibule as we came out."

"But if you had lost it in the street, we would have heard it fall. It must be in the cab."

"Yes. Did you notice the number?"

"No. Did you?"

"No."

They looked at each other, utterly cast down. Finally, Loisel started putting his clothes back on. "I'm going to retrace the route we took when we were walking."

And he went. She remained slumped in a chair in her evening gown, without ambition or thought, not even having the strength to go to bed.

Around seven o'clock her husband returned. He had not found it.

He went to the police and to the cab office, and put an advertisement in the newspapers, offering a reward. He did everything that offered them a suspicion of hope. She waited all day in a state of bewilderment at this frightful disaster.

Loisel returned in the evening with his face drawn and pale; he had discovered nothing. "What you must do," he said, "is write to your friend that you have broken the clasp of the necklace and are going to have it repaired. That will gain us some time."

She wrote as he dictated.

At the end of a week they had lost all hope. And Loisel, older by five years, declared: "We must find a way to replace the necklace."

The next day they took the black satin jewel case to the jeweler whose name was on the inside. He consulted his records. "It was not I, Madame," he said, "who sold this necklace. I only furnished the casket."[13]

Then they went from jeweler to jeweler, seeking a necklace like the other one, consulting their memories, and ill, both of them, with chagrin and anxiety.

In a shop in the Palais-Royal, they found a necklace of diamonds that looked just like the one they had lost. It was valued at forty thousand francs. They could get it for thirty-six thousand.

They begged the jeweler not to sell it for three days, and they made an arrangement whereby they could return it for thirty-four thousand francs if they found the other one before the end of February.

Loisel possessed eighteen thousand francs which his father had left him. He borrowed the rest. He borrowed it, asking for a thousand francs of one person, five hundred of another, five louis[14] of this one and three louis of that one. He gave I.O.U.'s, made ruinous promises, borrowed money from usurers and the whole race of lenders. He compromised his whole existence, in fact, risking his signature without even knowing whether he could make it good or not. And, harassed by fear for the future, by the black misery which surrounded him, and by the prospect of physical privation and moral torture, he went to get the new necklace, depositing on the merchant's counter thirty-six thousand francs.

When Mme. Loisel took the necklace back to Mme. Forestier, the latter said to her in a frigid tone, "You should have returned it to me sooner. I might have needed it."

She did not open the jewel-box as her friend had feared she would. If she had noticed the substitution, what would she have thought? Would she have taken her for a thief?

Mme. Loisel now knew a life of wretched poverty. She did her part, however, completely and heroically. It was necessary to pay this frightful debt. She would pay it. They let their maid go; they moved out of their lodgings and rented rooms in an attic.

She learned the heavy chores of a household, the odious work of a kitchen. She washed the dishes, using her rosy fingernails on the greasy pots and the bottoms of the saucepans. She washed the soiled linen, the shirts and dishtowels, and hung them on the line to dry. She took the trash down to the street each morning and brought up the water, stopping on each landing to catch her breath. And, clothed like a working-class woman, she went to the grocer's, the butcher's, and the fruiterer's with her basket on her arm, shopping, haggling, defending to the last sou[15] her miserable money.

Every month they had to pay some notes and renew others, so as to gain time. The husband worked evenings, putting the books of some merchants in order, and at night he often did copying at five sous a page.

And this life lasted for ten years.

At the end of the ten years they had repaid all, all, including the usurer's interest and compound interest besides.

Mme. Loisel looked old now. She had become a hard, strong woman, the crude woman of the poor household. Her hair badly dressed, her skirts awry, her hands red, she spoke in a loud voice and scrubbed the floors with large pails of water. But sometimes, when her husband was at the office, she would sit at the window and dream of that evening party long ago, of that ball where she was so beautiful and so flattered.

What would have happened if she had not lost that necklace? Who knows? How strange life is, and how full of changes! How small a thing will ruin or save one!

One Sunday, as she was taking a walk in the Champs-Elysees[16] to rid herself of the cares of the week, she suddenly saw a woman walking with a child. It was Mme. Forestier, still young, still pretty, still attractive. Mme. Loisel was strangely excited. Should she speak to her? Yes, certainly. And now that she had paid, she would tell her everything. Why not?

She approached her. "Good morning, Jeanne."

Her friend did not recognize her, and was surprised to be addressed so familiarly by this common-looking person. She stammered. "But, Madame—I don't know—you must be mistaken—"

"No. I am Matilda Loisel."

Her friend uttered a cry of astonishment. "Oh! My poor Matilda — how you have changed!"

"Yes, I have had some hard times since I saw you last, and some miserable ones — and all because of you."

"Because of me? What do you mean?"

"You remember the diamond necklace that you lent me to wear to the Commissioner's ball?"

"Yes, very well."

"Well, I lost it."

"But how could that be, since you returned it to me?"

"I returned another necklace that was just like it. And it has taken us ten years to pay for it. You can understand how hard it was for us who have nothing. But it's finished, and I am decently content."

Mme. Forestier stopped short. She said, "You say you bought a diamond necklace to replace mine?"

"Yes. You didn't notice it, then? They were exactly alike." And she smiled with a proud and simple joy.

Mme. Forestier was touched, and took both her friend's hands as she replied: "Oh, my poor Matilda! Mine were false. They were not worth over five hundred francs!"

1 **dowry:** money, goods, or property that a woman brings to her husband in marriage
2 **caste:** social class or rank
3 **finesse:** refinement; delicacy
4 **antechambers:** small rooms leading to larger ones; waiting rooms
5 **boudoirs:** private sitting rooms
6 **tapestries:** wall hangings made of heavy fabrics with designs woven into them
7 **gallantries:** compliments
8 **sphinx:** a mysterious or puzzling person
9 **francs:** French currency
10 **salons:** parlors; sitting rooms
11 **Seine:** a river in northern France. Paris is on the Seine.
12 **coupés:** horse-drawn carriages
13 **casket:** small box or chest used to hold jewels or other valuables
14 **louis:** former French gold coins worth 20 francs apiece
15 **sou:** former French coin worth 1/20 of a franc
16 **Champs-Elysees:** a famous boulevard in Paris

## A CLOSER LOOK

*1. What kind of person is Matilda? In your answer, discuss her values, the kinds of things that are important to her, and her feelings about not having them.*

*2. On whom does Matilda take out her dissatisfaction with her life? Do you think her complaints are justified? Why or why not?*

*3. The loss of the necklace is an unlucky accident, or twist of fate. Nevertheless, it can be argued that Matilda brought this fate upon herself. Explain why, using what you know about her character to support your answer.*

*4. The ending of the story is powerful because the news about the fake necklace comes as a complete surprise. But it is also powerful because de Maupassant stops right there, leaving us with the full impact of the surprise. Suppose he had gone on to describe Matilda's reaction to the news. Would the ending have been as powerful? Why or why not?*

• Gwendolyn Brooks is a poet. And, like all great poets, she sees the world in an imaginative way. So it's not surprising that in this story she turns a simple encounter with a mouse into an act of creation.

## Gwendolyn Brooks

# MAUD MARTHA SPARES THE MOUSE

THERE. SHE HAD IT AT LAST. THE WEEKS IT HAD devoted to eluding[1] her, the tricks, the clever hide-and-go-seeks, the routes it had in all sobriety[2] devised, together with the delicious moments it had, undoubtedly, laughed up its sleeve — all to no ultimate avail. She had that mouse.

It shook its little self, as best it could, in the trap. Its bright black eyes contained no appeal — the little creature seemed to understand that there was no hope of mercy from the eternal enemy, no hope of reprieve or postponement — but a fine small dignity. It waited. It looked at Maud Martha.

She wondered what else it was thinking. Perhaps that there was not enough food in its larder.[3] Perhaps that little Betty, a puny child from the start, would not, now, be getting fed. Perhaps that, now, the family's seasonal house-cleaning, for lack of expert direction, would be left undone. It might be regretting that young Bobby's education was now at an end. It might be nursing personal regrets. No more the mysterious shadows of the kitchenette, the uncharted twists, the unguessed halls. No more the sweet delights of the chase, the charms of being unsuccessfully hounded, thrown at.

Maud Martha could not bear the little look.

"Go home to your children," she urged. "To your wife or husband." She opened the trap. The mouse vanished.

Suddenly, she was conscious of a new cleanness in her. A wide air walked in her. A life had blundered its way into her power and it had been hers to preserve or destroy. She had not destroyed. In

31

the center of that simple restraint[4] was — creation. She had created a piece of life. It was wonderful.

"Why," she thought, as her height doubled, "why, I'm good! I am *good*."

She ironed her aprons. Her back was straight. Her eyes were mild, and soft with a godlike loving-kindness.

[1] **eluding:** avoiding or escaping by cleverness or quickness
[2] **sobriety:** seriousness
[3] **larder:** place where food is stored; pantry
[4] **restraint:** act of holding back

## A CLOSER LOOK

1. *What does Maud Martha see when she looks closely at the mouse's eyes? As she watches the mouse, what does she imagine it is thinking about?*

2. *When she first saw the mouse, Maud Martha thought of it as nothing more than a pesky rodent. How does she think of it now? Why does she decide to spare its life?*

3. *How does Maud Martha feel about herself after freeing the mouse? Quote the sentence in which she tells us. Now look at the sentence again and identify the phrase that gives us a visual image of her feeling.*

● To Uncle Leon, it was an irritating mistake. To Grandfather, it was outrageous. What they never suspected was that this particular mistake was really an act of kindness.

## Charles Einstein

# A FAVOR FOR LEFTY

N OUR FAMILY, WE HAVE AN EXPRESSION — "DO A favor for Lefty" — that, like the private sayings you have in your own family, is very hard to translate so outsiders will understand. Even today, a generation later, I am not as qualified as, say, my father, to use this expression with its exact nuance[1] and meaning (though I have used it time and time again) because I wasn't there when it happened. I was five years old, and five-year-olds don't go to funerals.

What happened was that Mr. Ghiblikian, who lived across the street from us in Boston, died. He died of old age. He was in his eighties, and he had had a long and a full life, and he died peacefully. My grandfather and my father and my Uncle Leon all went to the funeral parlor for the services, and they went in two cars. This was because Uncle Leon had bought a new car the day before, and he insisted on driving it every chance he got. My grandfather refused to drive anywhere in a car that had Uncle Leon behind the wheel, so Grandfather went with my father; and Uncle Leon went in his own car, a trifle bitterly.

"Why won't you go in the same car with me?" he'd asked Grandfather.

"Because you don't look at the road when you drive," Grandfather said.

"I have to look for the signs."

"You can't drive and look for signs at the same time," my grandfather said, and that was that.

Funeral services were held for Mr. Ghiblikian at one of the largest chapels in Boston, and after that all the cars got in line to follow the hearse to the cemetery. My father and my grandfather got back from the burial before Uncle Leon, and they were both upset about something. From their conversation, often recounted,[2] I have been able to reconstruct at least dimly what had happened.

"He did what you told him," my father said. "He stopped looking for signs and kept his eye on the road."

"So he got lost and never showed up at the cemetery!" Grandfather shouted. "A fine time to stop looking for signs!"

"Look," my father said. "There was a whole crowd of mourners. One more wasn't missed. And of the three of us — you and me and Leon — Leon knew Mr. Ghiblikian the least. It isn't as if he was as close to him as you were."

It was not typical of my father to stick up for Uncle Leon this way, but in later years I have understood that Grandfather was upset over the death of his friend and that my father was trying to soothe him.

He wasn't too successful. "Signs!" my grandfather shouted. "Signs! He didn't even have to look for signs! All he had to do was stay in line in the parade" — "parade" was not the right word for a funeral procession, but my grandfather did not know the right word and meant nothing disrespectful, and my father, wisely, did not correct him — "and he couldn't miss!"

"Maybe he had a flat tire," my father said.

"Brand-new car!" my grandfather bellowed. "It goes two miles, a flat tire?"

"He might have run over a nail."

"So while he's looking for signs he'll look for nails too!"

There was the sound of a key in the door. My Uncle Leon came in and found himself looking down the barrel of an accusing finger.

"You!" my grandfather bellowed at him.

My father said, "Leon, what happened?"

"It's hard to explain," Uncle Leon said.

"It's hard to explain," my grandfather said, in savage mimicry. "Your brother and I were at a funeral today. Where were you?"

"At a funeral," Leon said.

"You saw them bury Ghiblikian?" my grandfather asked doubtfully.

"No. I saw them bury somebody else."

"Who?"

"I don't know."

"I may hit him," my grandfather said to my father.

"It's very simple," Uncle Leon said. "I mean, it's not simple, but the way it worked out there wasn't anything else I could do." He looked appealingly at my father. "You know how the cars got jammed up on Beacon Street a few blocks away from the chapel?" My father nodded, looking carefully at my grandfather.

"Well, I guess I got in the wrong lane," Uncle Leon said. "The traffic started to move, and a cop waved me on through a light, and I saw I was right behind one of the chapel limousines, and right in front of the limousine was a hearse from the same chapel, so naturally I thought I'd moved up in the line and was following Mr. Ghiblikian's hearse." He shrugged. "Nobody told me where the cemetery was, anyway, so I had no way of knowing I was following a different hearse to a different cemetery."

"Seems only yesterday," my grandfather said to him, "you came home from the school saying, 'Papa, I got an A in American history.' What brains have you got? How come you ever got an A in anything?"

"There was just nothing I could do," Uncle Leon said. "The traffic was heavy, and I didn't recognize the people in the car behind me, but Mr. Ghiblikian knew a lot of people I didn't know, so that didn't mean anything; and you couldn't tell who was riding in the limousine in front of me. So" — he took a deep breath — "it wasn't till we turned in the cemetery gate and stopped at the graveside that I realized."

My father said, "Realized that you were at the wrong funeral?"

"Realized that I was the only car in that procession, besides the hearse and the limousine. I got out of the car and there was nobody

behind me. And all there was in the limousine up ahead was the widow and the minister and a man from the funeral parlor."

My grandfather stared at him. "So?"

"So what could I do?" Leon said plaintively. "I can't say I'm sorry, good-bye. I was in the presence of the dead. The minister came up and shook my hand. I had to stay where I was."

Nobody said anything for a time. Then Uncle Leon broke the silence. "The minister said his few words, and then it was over, and you know what happened? The widow came up and kissed me on the cheek. And you know what she said? She said, 'I know you don't want to tell me who you are, but you did my husband a favor, coming here today. I want to thank you,' she said."

And that was Uncle Leon's story, and that way it stood until the following morning, when the papers came and there was a little item that said:

*Small-time racketeer Lefty Brown, fatally wounded in a holdup attempt last Thursday, was buried at Fair View Cemetery yesterday, all but unmourned. Cemetery officials said only the widow, Mrs. Frances Brown, and an unidentified escort accompanied the body to its final resting place. . . .*

It all checked out. That unidentified escort was my Uncle Leon, and I guess the widow must have thought he was some hoodlum or other, which is why she told him she wouldn't ask his name.

And since that time we have this expression in our family — "Do a favor for Lefty." It is by no means a sardonic or sarcastic saying, but implies instead something unplanned but nonetheless warm: something that means some unexpected happiness in some unexpected direction, something that deals with fate. It is like the expressions you have come to have in your own family — there's no describing them or explaining them to outsiders.

You know how it is.

[1] **nuance:** subtle or slight distinction in meaning or tone
[2] **recounted:** told in detail

## A CLOSER LOOK

*1. To help us understand an old family expression, the narrator tells the story of how it began. Think about the story. Then explain what you think "Do a favor for Lefty" means.*

*2. Which character comes out on top in this story? Explain your answer.*

*3. Explain why the newspaper item about Lefty Brown is an important part of the story.*

*4. Instead of telling us what the characters are like, the author uses dialogue to reveal this information. Think about Father, Grandfather, and Uncle Leon. Then look through the story for an example of a conversation that helps us get to know one of them. Which character do we learn about in the conversation you have selected? What do we learn about him?*

● Like most science fiction writers, Michael Fedo bases his ideas about the future on conditions and trends that he observes in the present. In "The Carnival," he imagines a society in the 21st century that has faced the problem of overpopulation and solved it — in a bizarre way. But what is a solution for the society as a whole creates problems for individual members.

# Michael Fedo

# THE CARNIVAL

THE CHARTERED BUS STOPPED AT THE CORNER OF Fourteenth and Squire. Jerry smiled nervously, turned and waved to his mother, who stood weeping a few feet away, and boarded the bus.

He returned the driver's silent nod and settled himself in the only remaining seat — near the front — next to a poorly dressed middle-aged woman.

Jerry tingled with excitement. He glanced around, eager for conversation, but the other passengers were strangely silent. This puzzled Jerry, for he was looking forward with great anticipation to the carnival.

Indeed, he felt fortunate in having won the drawing at school which allowed him to attend the carnival free, as a special guest of the government. In an effort to encourage patronage[1] among young people, the government agency—Populace Control—sponsored drawings and contests for students.

The man and woman seated behind Jerry began talking about carnivals of years gone by — how they used to be very popular with kids, but weren't nearly as exciting as those of today. From the way they spoke, Jerry guessed they had attended many carnivals. He turned around and saw they were about the age of his parents.

How much more interesting than his parents they were, Jerry thought. His parents wouldn't dream of taking in the carnival, and Jerry sometimes wondered what they had to live for.

The couple noticed Jerry staring at them, and he coughed and faced the front. He squirmed in his seat.

The woman next to Jerry nudged him. "You don't look old enough," she said, looking straight ahead.

"I'm sixteen," Jerry responded sharply.

The woman turned toward him. "They never had these when I was sixteen. I wish they had."

"Why?"

The woman ignored him. "I hope today's my day," she sighed. "Oh, let it be today." She blew her nose into a crumpled handkerchief and stared out of the mud-splattered window.

The bus rolled past gray neighborhoods. Silent people on the streets, wearing distant, vacant faces, did not look up as the bus went by.

The bus joggled along with its silent passengers until it came to a stop in a part of town unfamiliar to Jerry.

The driver stood and faced the passengers. "All right, folks," he said. "This is it. Get your I.D. cards ready. The P.C. officer will be boarding in a minute. Those with government passes step to the front."

Jerry got up.

"You got a pass?" the woman next to him asked.

"Yes," Jerry said. "I won it at school."

The woman turned away again, and Jerry went to the front of the bus, where the Populace Control officer was standing.

"Just a second, boy," he said, as Jerry held out his identification and pass. "I have an announcement to make." The passengers listlessly raised their heads.

"As you know," he began, "some of you may not be making the return trip on this bus."

Jerry wished the officer would hurry. Didn't he know there was a carnival out there? Couldn't he tell that nobody wanted to hear him drone on and on? Well, hurry up, Jerry wanted to shout. Hurry up!

The man completed his memorized presentation and looked at Jerry, who was chewing his knuckles in impatience. "Take it easy, son," the officer said. "There's plenty of time — plenty of opportunity for everyone."

"Yes, sir," Jerry said.

He leaped from the bus as soon as the officer had punched his pass, and ran to join the clamoring throng at the carnival's main gate.

It was just the way he had pictured it. The bright lights, the

scuffling noises of the mass of moving people, the laughter and the shrieks of those who had dared board the death-defying rides.

Jerry's heartbeat quickened as he walked along the midway.

"First time, sonny?" an ancient carny[2] called to him. "Chance your life on this little spin, why don't you?"

Jerry gazed at the whirling machine high above his head. "I might later," he said.

"If you're lucky," the carny replied.

Jerry found himself being swept along with the crowd. Ahead of him a police officer was leading a young woman by the arm. She was sobbing and telling the officer she didn't want to leave her husband.

Jerry hardly noticed. He had more important things on his mind. He was attending his first carnival, and he had to make the most of it. He inhaled deeply, then reached into his pocket and clutched his pass.

The crush of the crowd took Jerry several hundred yards south of the main gate. Hundreds of attractions awaited the customers. Jerry sat down on a bench to study a map of the carnival grounds and decide which amusements he wanted to chance.

No sooner had he removed the map from his pocket than two burly men, struggling with something in a large plastic bag, passed him. They half-dragged their load to a huge pit and tossed it in.

Jerry wandered over to the edge of the pit. It was enormous — a hundred yards square and no telling how deep.

"The odds are one in eight you'll make it, kid," one of the men said with a crooked smile. "One in eight today." Both men laughed and walked away.

Jerry peered into the pit. There seemed to be a mountain of black plastic bags rising from the floor of the abyss.[3] Jerry shuddered briefly, then turned away.

He didn't look back, but sought cheerier sights instead — the flashing neon lights all about him. The spectacle was breathtaking. Jerry had never in his life been so excited. But then he had never known such cause for excitement, either.

He felt in his pocket for his pass and stopped for a drink from a water fountain, then continued along the midway.

The sky was darkening slightly, but Jerry didn't expect rain. The forecast had said no rain, and the Weather Control Center was never wrong.

Jerry got into the line of people who wanted to ride on the Thunder Clapper. In front of him stood a young man with glasses. He was sweating profusely,[4] although the temperature was on the cool side.

The young man glanced over his shoulder. "First time?" he asked, nervously rubbing his hands together.

"Yes," Jerry answered.

"Good luck," the man said. "This one's a real killer."

Jerry saw the contraption resting fifty feet ahead. "You ever been on it before?"

The man cleared his throat. "Nope. But I've gone on a lot of the other ones."

"This is my first ride," Jerry said.

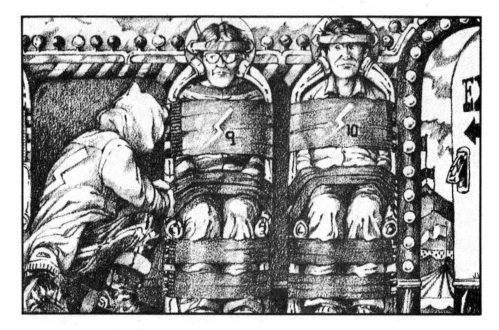

The young man laughed. "You sure picked a good one for a starter."

"I hope so," Jerry said.

The riders grew funereally silent as they came up to the boarding ramp. Jerry took a deep breath. He could feel his pulse in his throat. He stepped on to the ramp and selected a seat next to the young man he had met in the line.

An attendant came over and strapped them both in. The straps covered most of the body and were fastened very tightly. Jerry found breathing difficult.

"That'll hold you, Shorty," the attendant said, as he finished with Jerry. Jerry noticed that the attendant wore thick-soled boots and carried heavy gloves in his back pocket.

An announcement was made, stating that the ride would last only ninety seconds. It was everyone for himself. The announcer then wished the riders good luck, and the motor started.

It rumbled and coughed, then gained momentum as it lifted the apparatus and its occupants into the air. It picked up speed now, and the low rumble became a violent roar.

Jerry felt his stomach knot beneath the straps holding him. He hoped he wasn't going to be sick.

The roar was deafening. Jerry screamed, but no sound seemed to come from his lips. Lightning cracked all about him, coming so close he thought he could feel its intense heat.

Then suddenly the roar subsided, and the huge metal wheel was gently eased onto its base. The attendant unstrapped Jerry and the young man next to him. The young man didn't move, and two men came over to take him from the seat.

Jerry bounded quickly down the ramp. "I did it! I made it on my first try!" he shrieked, half-stumbling back onto the midway.

A uniformed statistician[5] smiled at Jerry's exuberance, and continued with his work. In the "Departure" column on the paper in front of him, he added another check.

Jerry wanted to shout his success; he wanted to run, but there was no room on the crowded midway.

What's so tough about this anyway? Jerry thought. If you take a positive approach, you'll overcome it.

He had easily met the challenge of this first ride — the one everybody had said would be the roughest. Well, he had come through, almost without flinching.

The taste of this kind of success was something he had not known before. He felt so exhilarated that he giggled in spite of himself.

He would try his luck again after he had had some food. He walked over to a refreshment stand and bought two hot dogs. "I've just been on the Thunder Clapper," he told the concessionaire.

"That's living pretty dangerously," the man said.

"Is there any other way?" Jerry asked lightly, paying for the food.

He ate rapidly, anxious to get back into action. Although he reveled[6] in his achievement, he knew that he could really prove his mettle[7] only by continuing to accept challenge. As soon as he had swallowed the last bite, he joined a red-haired boy about his own age in the line for the Whirl-Away.

The other boy smiled and told Jerry that this was to be his first ride.

"This is nothing," Jerry told him. "I've just come off the Thunder Clapper."

The red-haired boy's eyes widened with admiration. "I think this will be just as tough," he said, without conviction.

"I doubt it," Jerry scoffed. "But it'll probably help build your confidence."

The thrill-seekers were led to their places by Whirl-Away attendants, and strapped into the spokes of the machine in upright, standing positions.

Again there was an announcement over the public address system. It was the usual drivel that Jerry hardly heard.

Jerry was relaxed; a calm smile played over his lips. He settled back, ready to enjoy this new experience to the fullest.

The Whirl-Away began to vibrate, its engines whooshing like a great wind storm. The structure throbbed and gained speed until the passengers near the rim were moving at about two hundred miles an hour.

Jerry was thinking of the stories he'd tell his classmates at school tomorrow. How he took on the Thunder Clapper and the Whirl-Away, straight off. "You take the meanest ones first," he would tell them.

The Whirl-Away, spinning at an ever-increasing speed, rose three hundred feet off the ground.

Jerry became aware of a dizzy sensation. Then the sense of motion ceased, and suddenly he was free of movement and sound. He was in the air, hurtling headlong downward. "It isn't fair!" he tried to shout. "They said one in eight — one in eight!"

Men from the pit moved into position with their black plastic bags. But Jerry did not see them; nor was he conscious when he ceased to be — approaching the earth, meeting it face to face at almost the speed of sound.

[1] **patronage:** regular support or business from customers
[2] **carny:** one who works at a carnival
[3] **abyss:** bottomless pit
[4] **profusely:** with great abundance
[5] **statistician:** one who collects facts and figures about people or things
[6] **reveled:** took great pleasure in
[7] **mettle:** courage

## A CLOSER LOOK

*1. What government agency sponsors the carnival? What does this suggest about the purpose of the carnival?*

*2. Why do you think Jerry was so eager to go to the carnival?*

*3. Jerry's society takes advantage of a fairly widespread human trait: "the gambling instinct," or hunger for the thrill that comes from taking dangerous chances. The higher the stakes, the more attractive the game to people who enjoy this kind of excitement. What are the stakes at the carnival?*

● To most people, the word *heritage* brings to mind history, tradition, a legacy from the past. But to Alice Walker, heritage lives on in the present as well. And in "Everyday Use," she shows us the difference between people who live their heritage and those who merely talk about it.

## Alice Walker

# EVERYDAY USE

*for your grandmama*

I WILL WAIT FOR HER IN THE YARD THAT MAGGIE and I made so clean and wavy yesterday afternoon. A yard like this is more comfortable than most people know. It is not just a yard. It is like an extended living room. When the hard clay is swept clean as a floor and the fine sand around the edges lined with tiny, irregular grooves, anyone can come and sit and look up into the elm tree and wait for the breezes that never come inside the house.

Maggie will be nervous until after her sister goes: she will stand hopelessly in corners homely and ashamed of the burn scars down her arms and legs, eyeing her sister with a mixture of envy and awe. She thinks her sister has held life always in the palm of one hand, that "no" is a word the world never learned to say to her.

You've no doubt seen those TV shows where the child who has "made it" is confronted, as a surprise, by her own mother and father, tottering in weakly from backstage. (A pleasant surprise, of course: What would they do if parent and child came on the show only to curse out and insult each other?) On TV mother and child embrace and smile into each other's faces. Sometimes the mother and father weep, the child wraps them in her arms and leans across the table to tell how she would not have made it without their help. I have seen these programs.

Sometimes I dream a dream in which Dee and I are suddenly brought together on a TV program of this sort. Out of a dark and soft-seated limousine I am ushered into a bright room filled with many people. There I meet a smiling, gray, sporty man like Johnny Carson who shakes my hand and tells me what a fine girl I have. Then we are on the stage and Dee is embracing me with tears in her eyes. She pins on my dress a large orchid, even though she has told me once that she thinks orchids are tacky flowers.

In real life I am a large, big-boned woman with rough, man-working hands. In the winter I wear flannel nightgowns to bed and overalls during the day. I can kill and clean a hog as mercilessly as a man. My fat keeps me hot in zero weather. I can work all day, breaking ice to get water for washing. I can eat pork liver cooked over the open fire minutes after it comes steaming from the hog. One winter I knocked a bull calf straight in the brain between the eyes with a sledge hammer and had the meat hung up to chill before nightfall. But of course all this does not show on television. I am the way my daughter would want me to be: a hundred pounds lighter, my skin like an uncooked barley pancake. My hair glistens in the hot bright lights. Johnny Carson has much to do to keep up with my quick and witty tongue.

But that is a mistake. I know even before I wake up. Who ever knew a Johnson with a quick tongue? Who can even imagine me looking a strange white man in the eye? It seems to me I have talked to them always with one foot raised in flight, with my head turned in whichever way is farthest from them. Dee, though. She would always look anyone in the eye. Hesitation was no part of her nature.

"How do I look, Mama?" Maggie says, showing just enough of her thin body enveloped in pink skirt and red blouse for me to know she's there, almost hidden by the door.

"Come out into the yard," I say.

Have you ever seen a lame animal, perhaps a dog run over by some careless person rich enough to own a car, sidle[1] up to some-one who is ignorant enough to be kind to him? That is the way my Maggie walks. She has been like this, chin on chest, eyes on ground, feet in shuffle, ever since the fire that burned the other house to the ground.

Dee is lighter than Maggie, with nicer hair and a fuller figure. She's a woman now, though sometimes I forget. How long ago was it that the other house burned? Ten, twelve years? Sometimes I can still hear the flames and feel Maggie's arm sticking to me, her hair smoking and her dress falling off her in little black papery flakes.

Her eyes seemed stretched open, blazed open by the flames reflected in them. And Dee. I see her standing off under the sweet gum tree she used to dig gum out of; a look of concentration on her face as she watched the last dingy gray board of the house fall in toward the red-hot brick chimney. Why don't you do a dance around the ashes? I'd wanted to ask her. She had hated the house that much.

I used to think she hated Maggie, too. But that was before we raised the money, the church and me, to send her to Augusta to school. She used to read to us without pity; forcing words, lies, other folks' habits, whole lives upon us two, sitting trapped and ignorant underneath her voice. She washed us in a river of make-believe, burned us with a lot of knowledge we didn't necessarily need to know. Pressed us to her with the serious way she read, to shove us away at just the moment, like dimwits, we seemed about to understand.

Dee wanted nice things. A yellow organdy dress to wear to her graduation from high school; black pumps to match a green suit she'd made from an old suit somebody gave me. She was determined to stare down any disaster in her efforts. Her eyelids would not flicker for minutes at a time. Often I fought off the temptation to shake her. At sixteen she had a style of her own: and knew what style was.

I never had an education myself. After second grade the school was closed down. Don't ask me why: in 1927 colored asked fewer questions than they do now. Sometimes Maggie reads to me. She stumbles along good-naturedly but can't see well. She knows she is not bright. Like good looks and money, quickness passed her by. She will marry John Thomas (who has mossy teeth in an earnest face) and then I'll be free to sit here and I guess just sing church songs to myself. Although I never was a good singer. Never could carry a tune. I was always better at a man's job. I used to love to milk till I was hoofed in the side in '49. Cows are soothing and slow and don't bother you, unless you try to milk them the wrong way.

I have deliberately turned my back on the house. It is three rooms, just like the one that burned, except the roof is tin; they don't make shingle roofs any more. There are no real windows, just some holes cut in the sides, like the portholes in a ship, but not round and not square, with rawhide holding the shutters up on the outside. This house is in a pasture, too, like the other one. No doubt when Dee sees it she will want to tear it down. She wrote me once that no matter where we "choose" to live, she will manage to come see us. But she will never bring her friends. Maggie and I thought about this and Maggie asked me, "Mama, when did Dee ever *have* any friends?"

She had a few. Furtive[2] boys in pink shirts hanging about on washday after school. Nervous girls who never laughed. Impressed with her they worshiped the well-turned phrase, the cute shape, the scalding humor that erupted like bubbles in lye. She read to them.

When she was courting Jimmy T she didn't have much time to pay to us, but turned all her faultfinding power on him. He *flew* to marry a cheap gal from a family of ignorant flashy people. She hardly had time to recompose herself.

When she comes I will meet — but there they are!

Maggie attempts to make a dash for the house, in her shuffling way, but I stay her with my hand. "Come back here," I say. And she stops and tries to dig a well in the sand with her toe.

It is hard to see them clearly through the strong sun. But even the first glimpse of leg out of the car tells me it is Dee. Her feet were always neat-looking, as if God himself had shaped them with a certain style. From the other side of the car comes a short, stocky man. Hair is all over his head a foot long and hanging from his chin like a kinky mule tail. I hear Maggie suck in her breath. "Uhnnnh," is what it sounds like. Like when you see the wriggling end of a snake just in front of your foot on the road. "Uhnnnh."

Dee next. A dress down to the ground, in this hot weather. A dress so loud it hurts my eyes. There are yellows and oranges enough to throw back the light of the sun. I feel my whole face warming from the heat waves it throws out. Earrings, too, gold and hanging down to her shoulders. Bracelets dangling and making noises when she moves her arm up to shake the folds of the dress out of her armpits. The dress is loose and flows, and as she walks closer, I like it. I hear Maggie go "Uhnnnh" again. It is her sister's hair. It stands straight up like the wool on a sheep. It is black as night and around the edges are two long pigtails that rope about like small lizards disappearing behind her ears.

"Wa-su-zo-Tean-o!" she says, coming on in that gliding way the dress makes her move. The short stocky fellow with the hair to his navel is all grinning and he follows up with "Asalamalakim, my mother and sister!" He moves to hug Maggie but she falls back, right up against the back of my chair. I feel her trembling there and when I look up I see the perspiration falling off her chin.

"Don't get up," says Dee. Since I am stout it takes something of a push. You can see me trying to move a second or two before I make it. She turns, showing white heels through her sandals, and goes back to the car. Out she peeks next with a Polaroid. She stoops down quickly and lines up picture after picture of me sitting there in front of the house with Maggie cowering behind me. She never takes a shot without making sure the house is included. When a cow comes nibbling around the edge of the yard she snaps it and me and Maggie *and* the house. Then she puts the Polaroid in the back seat of the car, and comes up and kisses me on the forehead.

Meanwhile Asalamalakim is going through the motions with Maggie's hand. Maggie's hand is as limp as a fish, and probably as cold, despite the sweat, and she keeps trying to pull it back. It looks like Asalamalakim wants to shake hands but wants to do it fancy. Or maybe he don't know how people shake hands. Anyhow, he soon gives up on Maggie.

"Well," I say. "Dee."

"No, Mama," she says. "Not 'Dee,' Wangero Leewanika Kemanjo!"

"What happened to 'Dee'?" I wanted to know.

"She's dead," Wangero said. "I couldn't bear it any longer being named after the people who oppress me."

"You know as well as me you was named after your aunt Dicie," I said. Dicie is my sister. She named Dee. We called her "Big Dee" after Dee was born.

"But who was *she* named after?" asked Wangero.

"I guess after Grandma Dee," I said.

"And who was she named after?" asked Wangero.

"Her mother," I said, and saw Wangero was getting tired. "That's about as far back as I can trace it," I said. Though, in fact, I probably could have carried it back beyond the Civil War through the branches.

"Well," said Asalamalakim, "there you are."

"Uhnnnh," I heard Maggie say.

"There I was not," I said, "before 'Dicie' cropped up in our family, so why should I try to trace it that far back?"

He just stood there grinning, looking down on me like somebody inspecting a Model A car. Every once in a while he and
Wangero sent eye signals over my head.

"How do you pronounce this name?" I asked.

"You don't have to call me by it if you don't want to," said
Wangero.

"Why shouldn't I?" I asked. "If that's what you want us to call
you, we'll call you."

"I know it might sound awkward at first," said Wangero.

"I'll get used to it," I said. "Ream it out again."

Well, soon we got the name out of the way. Asalamalakim had a
name twice as long and three times as hard. After I tripped over it
two or three times he told me just call him Hakim-a-barber. I
wanted to ask him was he a barber, but I didn't really think he was,
so I didn't ask.

"You must belong to those beef-cattle peoples down the road," I
said. They said "Asalamalakim" when they met you, too, but they
didn't shake hands. Always too busy: feeding the cattle, fixing the
fences, putting up salt-lick shelters, throwing down hay. When the
white folks poisoned some of the herd the men stayed up all night
with rifles in their hands. I walked a mile and a half just to see the
sight.

Hakim-a-barber said, "I accept some of their doctrines,[3] but
farming and raising cattle is not my style." (They didn't tell me,
and I didn't ask, whether Wangero [Dee] had really gone and
married him.)

We sat down to eat and right away he said he didn't eat collards
and pork was unclean. Wangero, though, went on through the
chitlins and corn bread, the greens and everything else. She talked
a blue streak over the sweet potatoes. Everything delighted her.
Even the fact that we still used the benches her daddy made for the
table when we couldn't afford to buy chairs.

"Oh, Mama!" she cried. Then turned to Hakim-a-barber. "I
never knew how lovely these benches are. You can feel the rump
prints," she said, running her hands underneath her and along the
bench. Then she gave a sigh and her hand closed over Grandma
Dee's butter dish. "That's it!" she said. "I knew there was something I wanted to ask you if I could have." She jumped up from the
table and went over in the corner where the churn[4] stood, the milk
in its clabber[5] by now. She looked at the churn and looked at it.

"This churn top is what I need," she said. "Didn't Uncle Buddy

50

whittle[6] it out of a tree you all used to have?"

"Yes," I said.

"Uh huh," she said happily. "And I want the dasher,[7] too."

"Uncle Buddy whittle that, too?" asked the barber.

Dee (Wangero) looked up at me.

"Aunt Dee's first husband whittled the dash," said Maggie so low you almost couldn't hear her. "His name was Henry, but they called him Stash."

"Maggie's brain is like an elephant's," Wangero said, laughing. "I can use the churn top as a centerpiece for the alcove table," she said, sliding a plate over the churn, "and I'll think of something artistic to do with the dasher."

When she finished wrapping the dasher the handle stuck out. I took it for a moment in my hands. You didn't even have to look close to see where hands pushing the dasher up and down to make butter had left a kind of sink in the wood. In fact, there were a lot of small sinks; you could see where thumbs and fingers had sunk into the wood. It was beautiful light yellow wood, from a tree that grew in the yard where Big Dee and Stash had lived.

After dinner Dee (Wangero) went to the trunk at the foot of my bed and started rifling through it. Maggie hung back in the kitchen over the dishpan. Out came Wangero with two quilts. They had been pieced by Grandma Dee and then Big Dee and me had hung them on the quilt frames on the front porch and quilted them. One was in the Lone Star pattern. The other was Walk Around the Mountain. In both of them were scraps of dresses Grandma Dee had worn fifty and more years ago. Bits and pieces of Grandpa Jarrell's Paisley shirts. And one teeny faded blue piece, about the size of a penny matchbox, that was from Great Grandpa Ezra's

uniform that he wore in the Civil War.

"Mama," Wangero said sweet as a bird. "Can I have these old quilts?"

I heard something fall in the kitchen, and a minute later the kitchen door slammed.

"Why don't you take one or two of the others?" I asked. "These old things was just done by me and Big Dee from some tops your grandma pieced before she died."

"No," said Wangero. "I don't want those. They are stitched around the borders by machine."

"That's made them last better," I said.

"That's not the point," said Wangero. "These are all pieces of dresses Grandma used to wear. She did all this stitching by hand. Imagine!" She held the quilts securely in her arms, stroking them.

"Some of the pieces, like those lavender ones, come from old clothes her mother handed down to her," I said, moving up to touch the quilts. Dee (Wangero) moved back just enough so that I couldn't reach the quilts. They already belonged to her.

"Imagine!" she breathed again, clutching them closely to her bosom.

"The truth is," I said, "I promised to give them quilts to Maggie, for when she marries John Thomas."

She gasped like a bee had stung her.

"Maggie can't appreciate these quilts!" she said. "She'd probably be backward enough to put them to everyday use."

"I reckon she would," I said. "God knows I been saving 'em for long enough with nobody using 'em. I hope she will!" I didn't want to bring up how I had offered Dee (Wangero) a quilt when she went away to college. Then she had told me they were old-fashioned, out of style.

"But they're *priceless*!" she was saying now, furiously; for she has a temper. "Maggie would put them on the bed and in five years they'd be in rags. Less than that!"

"She can always make some more," I said. "Maggie knows how to quilt."

Dee (Wangero) looked at me with hatred. "You just will not understand. The point is these quilts, *these* quilts!"

"Well," I said, stumped. "What would *you* do with them?"

"Hang them," she said. As if that was the only thing you *could* do with quilts.

Maggie by now was standing in the door. I could almost hear the sound her feet made as they scraped over each other.

"She can have them, Mama," she said, like somebody used to never winning anything, or having anything reserved for her. "I can 'member Grandma Dee without the quilts."

I looked at her hard. She had filled her bottom lip with checker-berry snuff and it gave her face a kind of dopey, hangdog look. It was Grandma Dee and Big Dee who taught her how to quilt her-self. She stood there with her scarred hands hidden in the folds of her skirt. She looked at her sister with something like fear but she wasn't mad at her. This was Maggie's portion. This was the way she knew God to work.

When I looked at her like that something hit me in the top of my head and ran down to the soles of my feet. Just like when I'm in church and the spirit of God touches me and I get happy and shout. I did something I never had done before: hugged Maggie to me, then dragged her on into the room, snatched the quilts out of Miss Wangero's hands and dumped them into Maggie's lap. Maggie just sat there on my bed with her mouth open.

"Take one or two of the others," I said to Dee.

But she turned without a word and went out to Hakim-a-barber.

"You just don't understand," she said, as Maggie and I came out to the car.

"What don't I understand?" I wanted to know.

"Your heritage," she said. And then she turned to Maggie, kissed her, and said, "You ought to try to make something of yourself, too, Maggie. It's really a new day for us. But from the way you and Mama still live you'd never know it."

She put on some sunglasses that hid everything above the tip of her nose and her chin.

Maggie smiled; maybe at the sunglasses. But a real smile, not scared. After we watched the car dust settle I asked Maggie to bring me a dip of snuff. And then the two of us sat there just enjoying, until it was time to go in the house and go to bed.

---

[1] **sidle:** move sideways slowly so as not to attract attention
[2] **furtive:** marked by secrecy or slyness
[3] **doctrines:** the teachings or beliefs of a group of people
[4] **churn:** a container in which butter is made from cream or milk by beating and shaking
[5] **clabber:** thick, sour milk
[6] **whittle:** to shape something out of wood with a knife
[7] **dasher:** a plunger with paddles at one end used for stirring and mixing in a churn

## A CLOSER LOOK

*1. In the beginning of the story, the mother relates a dream she sometimes has of being brought together with Dee on a television program. From her description of that dream, what do we learn about the way she sees herself? What do we learn about the way Dee sees her?*

*2. How did Dee feel about her family and her background when she was growing up? During her visit, Dee seems delighted by some of the very things she once scorned—things she now sees as fashionable. Give an example of something that Dee once rejected but now wants to possess.*

*3. Do you think Dee wants Grandma's quilts because she values the heritage they represent? Or does she want the quilts because she sees them as status symbols? Support your answer with evidence from the story.*

*4. Reread the dialogue between Dee and her mother on page 53. Which statements reflect the author's belief that heritage is a living thing, kept alive through everyday use? Who makes those statements?*

*5. Maggie and Dee both share the same heritage. The quilt and Grandma Dee are part of that heritage. Maggie knows how to quilt; Dee doesn't. Maggie has loving memories of her grandmother. Dee has rejected her grandmother's name. Who is more likely to keep their heritage alive—Maggie or Dee? Explain your answer.*

*6. After saying that Dee can have the quilts, Maggie looks at her sister with "something like fear," but not anger. Her mother feels Maggie's loving spirit, just as she feels the loving spirit of God when she is in church. She also sees, perhaps for the first time, Maggie's inner strength. Why does this make her decide to give Maggie the quilt? How does Dee feel about her mother's decision? How does Maggie feel about it?*

• Imagine this: You are about to walk into the supermarket when you realize that you forgot your wallet. So you go home, planning to do your shopping the next day. What you don't know is that the ten-thousandth customer to enter the store will receive a gift certificate for a year's worth of free groceries. And you would have been that customer if you had gone into the supermarket. Without ever knowing it existed, you missed the opportunity of a lifetime. Nathaniel Hawthorne says that there are countless such "might-have-beens" in all our lives that we are never aware of. And he says it's just as well that we don't know what we're missing, because if we did know, we would all be nervous wrecks!

# Nathaniel Hawthorne

# DAVID SWAN

**W**E CAN BE ONLY PARTIALLY ACQUAINTED even with the events which actually influence our course through life, and our final destiny. There are innumerable other events — if such they may be called — which come close to us, yet pass by without actually touching us or even betraying their near approach by the reflection of any light or shadow across our minds. If we were aware of all the vicissitudes[1] of our fortunes, life would be too full of hope and fear, exultation or disappointment, to afford us a single hour of true serenity.[2] This idea may be illustrated by a page from the secret history of David Swan.

We have nothing to do with David until we find him, at the age of twenty, on the high road from his birthplace to the city of Boston, where his uncle, the owner of a small grocery store, was to employ him as a clerk behind the counter. Suffice it to say that he was a native of New Hampshire, born of respectable parents, and had received an ordinary school education, with a classic finish by a year at Gilmanton Academy.

After journeying on foot from sunrise till nearly noon of a summer's day, his weariness and the increasing heat made him decide to sit down in the first convenient shade and await the

coming of the stagecoach. As if planted on purpose for him, there soon appeared a little tuft of maples, with a delightful recess in the midst, and a spring so fresh and bubbling that it seemed never to have sparkled for any wayfarer but David Swan. He kissed it with his thirsty lips and then flung himself down on the brink, pillowing his head upon some shirts and a pair of pantaloons that he had tied up in a striped cotton handkerchief.

The sunbeams could not reach him, the dust had not yet begun to rise from the road after the heavy rain of yesterday, and his grassy lair[3] suited the young man better than a bed of down. The spring murmured drowsily beside him; the branches waved dreamily across the blue sky overhead; and a deep sleep, perchance hiding dreams within its depths, fell upon David Swan. But we will relate events which he did not dream of.

While he lay sound asleep in the shade, other people were wide awake, and they passed to and fro, afoot, on horseback, and in all sorts of vehicles, along the sunny road by his bedchamber. Some looked neither to the right hand nor the left, and knew not that he was there. Some merely glanced that way, without letting the slumberer enter their busy thoughts. Some laughed to see how soundly he slept. And several, whose hearts were brimming full of scorn, poured their venomous[4] overflow on David Swan. A middle-aged widow, when nobody else was near, thrust her head a little way into the recess, and vowed that the young fellow looked charming in his sleep. A temperance lecturer[5] saw him, and worked poor David into the speech he was to give that evening, as an awful example of dead drunkenness by the roadside. But censure,[6] praise, merriment, scorn, and indifference were all one, or

57

rather all nothing, to David Swan.

He had slept only a few moments when a brown carriage, drawn by a handsome pair of horses, bowled easily along, and was brought to a standstill nearly in front of David's resting place. A linchpin[7] had fallen out and permitted one of the wheels to slide off. The damage was slight and caused merely a momentary alarm to an elderly merchant and his wife, who were returning to Boston in the carriage.

While the coachman and a servant were replacing the wheel, the lady and the gentleman sheltered themselves beneath the maple trees, and there spied the bubbling fountain and David Swan asleep beside it. Impressed by the awe which the humblest sleeper usually sheds around him, the merchant trod as lightly as the gout[8] would allow; and his spouse took good heed not to rustle her silk gown, lest David should suddenly start up.

"How soundly he sleeps!" whispered the old gentleman. "From what a depth he draws that easy breath! Such sleep as that, brought on without any drug, would be worth more to me than half my income, because it proceeds from health and an untroubled mind."

"And from youth, besides," said the lady. "Age, even healthy and quiet age, does not sleep thus. Our slumber is no more like his than our wakefulness."

The longer they looked, the more did this elderly couple feel interested in the unknown youth, to whom the wayside and the maple shade were like a secret chamber, with the rich gloom of damask curtains brooding over him. Perceiving that a stray sunbeam glimmered down upon his face, the lady contrived to twist a branch aside, so as to intercept it. And having done this little act of kindness, she began to feel like a mother to him.

"Providence[9] seems to have laid him here," whispered she to her husband, "and to have brought us hither to find him, after our disappointment in our cousin's son. Methinks I can see a likeness to our departed Henry. Shall we waken him?"

"To what purpose?" said the merchant. "We know nothing of his character."

"That open countenance!"[10] replied his wife, in the same hushed voice, yet earnestly. "This innocent sleep!"

While these whispers were passing, the sleeper's heart did not throb, nor his breath become agitated, nor his features betray the least token of interest. Yet Fortune was bending over him, just

ready to let fall a burden of gold. The old merchant had lost his
only son and had no heir to his wealth except a distant relative,
with whose conduct he was dissatisfied. In such cases, people
sometimes do stranger things than to act the magician, and awaken
a young man to splendor who fell asleep in poverty.

"Shall we not waken him?" repeated the lady, persuasively.

"The coach is ready, sir," said the servant, behind.

The old couple started, reddened, and hurried away, both won-
dering how they could ever have dreamed of doing anything so
very ridiculous. The merchant leaned back in the carriage and
occupied his mind with plans for a magnificent asylum[11] for unfor-
tunate men of business. Meanwhile, David Swan enjoyed his nap.

The carriage could not have gone more than a mile or two when
a pretty young girl came along, walking at a tripping pace which
showed precisely how her little heart was dancing in her bosom.
Perhaps it was this merry gait that caused — is there any harm in
saying it? — her garter to slip its knot. Conscious that the silken
band — if silk it were — was relaxing its hold, she turned aside

into the shelter of the maple trees and there found a young man asleep by the spring!

Blushing as red as any rose that she should have intruded into a gentleman's bedchamber — and for such a purpose, too — she was about to make her escape on tiptoe. But there was peril near the sleeper. A monster of a bee had been wandering overhead — buzz, buzz, buzz — now among the leaves, now flashing through the strips of sunshine and now lost in the dark shade, till finally he appeared to be settling on David Swan's eyelid. The sting of the bee is sometimes deadly. As warmhearted as she was innocent, the girl attacked the intruder with her handkerchief, brushed him soundly, and drove him from beneath the maple shade. How sweet a picture! This good deed accomplished, with quickened breath and a deeper blush, she stole a glance at the youthful stranger for whom she had been battling with a dragon in the air.

"He is handsome!" thought she.

How could it be that no dream of bliss grew so strong within him that, shattered by its own strength, it should part asunder[12] and allow him to see the girl among its phantoms[13]? Why, at least, did no smile of welcome brighten upon his face? She had come, the girl whose soul (according to the old and beautiful idea) had been severed from his own, and whom, in all his vague but passionate desires, he yearned to meet. Her, only, could he love with a perfect love; him, only, could she receive into the depths of her heart. And now her image was faintly blushing in the fountain by his side. If it passed away, its happy luster would never gleam upon his life again.

"How sound he sleeps!" murmured the girl.

She departed, but did not trip along the road so lightly as when she came.

Now, this girl's father was a thriving country merchant in the neighborhood, and happened at that very time to be looking out for just such a young man as David Swan. Had David formed a wayside acquaintance with the daughter, he would have become the father's clerk, and everything else would have followed in the natural course of events. So here, again, good fortune — the best of fortunes — had stolen so near that her garments brushed against him, and he knew nothing about it.

The girl was hardly out of sight when two men turned aside beneath the maple shade. Both had dark faces, set off by cloth caps which were drawn down aslant over their foreheads. Their clothes were shabby, yet had a certain smartness. These were a couple of rascals who got their living by whatever the devil sent them and who now, during a pause in business, had staked the joint profits of their next piece of villainy on a game of cards, which was to be decided here under the trees. But, finding David asleep by the spring, one of the rogues whispered —

"Hsst! Do you see that bundle under his head?"

The other villain nodded, winked, and leered.

"I'll bet you a mug of brandy," said the first, "that the chap has either a pocketbook or a snug little hoard of small change stowed away amongst his shirts. And if it's not there, we shall find it in his pantaloons pockets."

"But what if he wakes?" said the other.

His companion opened his vest, pointed to the handle of a dagger, and nodded.

"So be it!" muttered the second villain.

They approached the unconscious David, and while one pointed the dagger at his heart the other began to search the bundle beneath his head. Their two faces, grim, wrinkled, and ghastly with guilt and fear, bent over their victim, looking horrible enough to be mistaken for fiends should he suddenly awake. Nay, if the villains had glanced aside into the spring, even they would hardly have known themselves as reflected there.

"I must take away the bundle," whispered one.

"If he stirs, I'll strike," muttered the other.

But at this moment a dog, sniffing along the ground, came in beneath the maple trees, and gazed at each of these wicked men in turn, and then at the quiet sleeper. He then lapped water out of the fountain.

"Pshaw!" said one villain. "We can do nothing now. The dog's master must be close behind."

"Let's take a drink and be off," said the other.

The man with the dagger thrust it back under his vest and drew forth a pocket pistol, but not of that kind which kills by a single discharge. It was a flask of liquor, with a tin cup screwed over the mouth. Each drank a comfortable dram and they left the spot, with so many jests and such laughter at their unaccomplished wickedness that they might be said to have gone on their way rejoicing. In a few hours they had forgotten the whole affair, nor did they even once imagine that the recording angel had written down the crime of murder against their souls, in letters as durable as eternity. As for David Swan, he still slept quietly, neither conscious of the shadow of death when it hung over him, nor of the glow of renewed life when that shadow was withdrawn.

He slept, but no longer so quietly as at first. An hour's repose had snatched from his elastic frame the weariness with which many hours of toil had burdened it. Now he stirred, now moved his lips without a sound, now talked, in an inward tone, to the noonday specters[14] of his dream. But the noise of wheels came rattling louder and louder along the road, until it dashed through the dispersing mist of David's slumber — and there was the stagecoach.

"Halloo, driver! Take a passenger?" shouted he.

"Room on top!" answered the driver.

Up mounted David and bowled away merrily toward Boston, without so much as a parting glance at that fountain of dreamlike vicissitude. He knew not that a phantom of Wealth had thrown a golden hue upon its waters, nor that one of Love had sighed softly to their murmur, nor that one of Death had threatened to crimson[15] them with his blood — all in the brief hour since he lay down to sleep.

Sleeping or waking, we hear not the airy footsteps of the strange things that almost happen. Yet, even though unseen and unexpected events thrust themselves continually across our path, there is still enough regularity in mortal life to make some foresight[16] possible.

Does this not suggest that there is a superintending Providence that guides us?

[1] **vicissitudes:** changes in circumstances
[2] **serenity:** peace and quiet; calmness
[3] **lair:** resting or sleeping place
[4] **venomous:** poisonous
[5] **temperance lecturer:** one who lectures on the evils of alcohol
[6] **censure:** blame; disapproval
[7] **linchpin:** a pin inserted in an axle to keep the wheel on
[8] **gout:** painful disease of the joints
[9] **Providence:** divine guidance or care
[10] **countenance:** face; expression
[11] **asylum:** a place of retreat and security; a shelter
[12] **asunder:** in pieces; into separate parts
[13] **phantoms:** spirits
[14] **specters:** visions
[15] **crimson:** turn deep red
[16] **foresight:** careful thought for the future; looking ahead

## A CLOSER LOOK

*1. In the first episode, why is the elderly couple tempted to wake David? Suppose David had awakened in their presence. What do we assume would have happened to him?*

*2. In the episode about the young woman, Hawthorne tells us that there is only one perfect mate for each of us. What opportunity does the young woman miss by not waking David? What two opportunities does David miss in this episode?*

*3. In the third episode waking up would have cost David his life. Explain why.*

*4. Hawthorne felt that we are better off not knowing about the things that might have happened to us. Do you agree? Pick one episode in the story and think about how David would feel if he knew what might have happened to him. Which do you think would be better for him: knowing or not knowing?*

*5. Hawthorne has David sleep through each episode to illustrate the opportunities and narrow escapes in life that we are never aware of. But at the end of the story, he says we also have opportunities that we do know about. And whether or not we take advantage of them is up to us. Think about the people who came upon David while he was sleeping. Which ones passed up opportunities that they knew about? What were those opportunities?*

# PART II

# SETTING

Every reader knows that the setting of a story is more than just "the place where it happens." The period of history in which it occurs is important, too, because each period is marked by a unique combination of political and social conditions that shape the characters' lives. In some stories, even the characters themselves are crucial factors in the environment. Have you ever been in an ordinary place that suddenly seemed beautiful to you because of the people you were with? If so, you will probably agree that human beings may often be as much a part of the setting as mountains, buildings, and trees.

Since a story has to take place somewhere and sometime, it is safe to say that the setting is an essential element in every story. But an element can be essential without being very important. In some stories it seems that the events could have occurred in many other settings besides the one chosen by the author. In others, however, the setting determines what can and cannot happen.

As you read the stories in this section, notice the important part that setting plays in each one. The train station shown in the picture at left is an example of the kind of setting that could be a crucial factor in a story. (As you probably noticed, the train station is part of the picture on pages 4-5.)

● To what lengths will a man go in search of revenge? Read this chilling tale by a master of suspense and find out.

# Edgar Allan Poe

# THE CASK OF AMONTILLADO

THE THOUSAND INJURIES OF FORTUNATO I HAD borne as I best could; but when he ventured upon insult, I vowed revenge. You, who so well know the nature of my soul, will not suppose, however, that I gave utterance to a threat. *At length* I would be avenged; this was a point definitively settled — but the very definitiveness with which it was resolved, precluded the idea of risk. I must not only punish, but punish with impunity.[1] A wrong is unredressed[2] when retribution[3] overtakes its redresser. It is equally unredressed when the avenger fails to make himself felt as such to him who has done the wrong.

It must be understood, that neither by word nor deed had I given Fortunato cause to doubt my good-will. I continued, as was my wont, to smile in his face, and he did not perceive that my smile *now* was at the thought of his immolation.[4]

He had a weak point — this Fortunato — although in other regards he was a man to be respected and even feared. He prided himself on his connoisseurship[5] in wine. Few Italians have the true virtuoso[6] spirit. For the most part their enthusiasm is adopted to suit the time and opportunity — to practice imposture upon the British and Austrian *millionaires.* In painting and gemmary Fortunato, like his countrymen, was a quack — but in the matter of old wines he was sincere. In this respect I did not differ from him materially: I was skillful in the Italian vintages myself, and bought largely whenever I could.

It was about dusk, one evening during the supreme madness of the carnival[7] season, that I encountered my friend. He accosted me with excessive warmth, for he had been drinking much. The man wore motley.[8] He had on a tight-fitting partistriped costume, and his head was surmounted by the conical cap and bells. I was so pleased to see him, that I thought I should never have done wringing his hand.

I said: "My dear Fortunato, you are luckily met. How well you are looking today! But I have received a pipe[9] of what passes for Amontillado,[10] and I have my doubts."

"How?" said he. "Amontillado? A pipe? Impossible! And in the middle of the carnival!"

"I have my doubts," I replied; "and I was silly enough to pay the full Amontillado price without consulting you in the matter. You were not to be found, and I was fearful of losing a bargain."

"Amontillado!"

"I have my doubts."

"Amontillado!"

"And I must satisfy them."

"Amontillado!"

"As you are engaged, I am on my way to Luchesi. If anyone has a critical turn, it is he. He will tell me — "

"Luchesi cannot tell Amontillado from Sherry."

"And yet some fools will have it that his taste is a match for your own."

"Come, let us go."

"Whither?"

"To your vaults."

"My friend, no; I will not impose upon your good nature. I perceive you have an engagement. Luchesi — "

"I have no engagement — come."

"My friend, no. It is not the engagement, but the severe cold with which I perceive you are afflicted. The vaults are insufferably damp. They are encrusted with nitre."[11]

"Let us go, nevertheless. The cold is merely nothing. Amontillado! You have been imposed upon. And as for Luchesi, he cannot distinguish Sherry from Amontillado."

Thus speaking, Fortunato possessed himself of my arm. Putting on a mask of black silk, and drawing a *roquelaure*[12] closely about my person, I suffered him to hurry me to my palazzo.

There were no attendants at home; they had absconded[13] to make merry in honor of the time. I had told them that I should not return until the morning, and had given them explicit orders not to stir from the house. These orders were sufficient, I well knew, to insure their immediate disappearance, one and all, as soon as my back was turned.

I took from their sconces two flambeaux,[14] and giving one to Fortunato, bowed him through several suites of rooms to the archway that led into the vaults. I passed down a long and winding staircase, requesting him to be cautious as he followed. We came at length to the foot of the descent, and stood together on the damp ground of the catacombs[15] of the Montresors.

The gait of my friend was unsteady, and the bells upon his cap jingled as he strode.

"The pipe?" said he.

"It is farther on," said I; "but observe the white web-work which gleams from these cavern walls."

He turned toward me, and looked into my eyes with two filmy orbs[16] that distilled the rheum[17] of intoxication.

"Nitre?" he asked, at length.

"Nitre," I replied. "How long have you had that cough?"

"Ugh! ugh! ugh! — ugh! ugh! ugh! — ugh! ugh! ugh! — ugh! ugh! ugh! — ugh! ugh! ugh!"

My poor friend found it impossible to reply for many minutes.

"It is nothing," he said, at last.

"Come," I said with decision, "we will go back; your health is precious. You are rich, respected, admired, beloved; you are happy, as once I was. You are a man to be missed. For me it is no matter. We will go back; you will be ill, and I cannot be responsible. Besides, there is Luchesi — "

"Enough," he said; "the cough is a mere nothing; it will not kill me. I shall not die of a cough."

"True — true," I replied; "and, indeed, I had no intention of alarming you unnecessarily; but you should use all proper caution. A draught of this Medoc will defend us from the damps."

Here I knocked off the neck of a bottle which I drew from a long row of its fellows that lay upon the mold.

"Drink," I said, presenting him the wine.

He raised it to his lips with a leer. He paused and nodded to me familiarly, while his bells jingled.

"I drink," he said, "to the buried that repose around us."

"And I to your long life."

He again took my arm, and we proceeded.

"These vaults," he said, "are extensive."

"The Montresors," I replied, "were a great and numerous family."

"I forget your arms."[18]

"A huge human foot d'or, in a field azure; the foot crushes a serpent rampant whose fangs are imbedded in the heel."[19]

"And the motto?"

"*Nemo me impune lacessit.*"[20]

"Good!" he said.

The wine sparkled in his eyes and the bells jingled. My own fancy grew warm with the Medoc. We had passed through walls of piled bones, with casks and puncheons[21] intermingling, into the inmost recesses of the catacombs. I paused again, and this time I made bold to seize Fortunato by an arm above the elbow.

"The nitre!" I said; "see, it increases. It hangs like moss upon the vaults. We are below the river's bed. The drops of moisture trickle among the bones. Come, we will go back ere it is too late. Your cough — "

"It is nothing," he said; "let us go on. But first, another draught of the Medoc."

I broke and reached him a flagon of De Grâve. He emptied it at a breath. His eyes flashed with a fierce light. He laughed and threw the bottle upward with a gesticulation I did not understand.

I looked at him in surprise.

"You do not comprehend?" he said.

"Not I," I replied.

"Then you are not of the brotherhood."

"How?"

"You are not of the masons."[22]

"Yes, yes," I said; "yes, yes."

"You? Impossible! A mason?"

"A mason," I replied.

"A sign," he said.

"It is this," I answered, producing a trowel[23] from beneath the folds of my *roquelaure*.

"You jest," he exclaimed, recoiling a few paces. "But let us proceed to the Amontillado."

"Be it so," I said, replacing the tool beneath the cloak, and again offering him my arm. He leaned upon it heavily. We continued our route in search of the Amontillado. We passed through a range of low arches, descended, passed on, and descending again, arrived at a deep crypt,[24] in which the foulness of the air caused our flambeaux rather to glow than flame.

At the most remote end of the crypt there appeared another less spacious. Its walls had been lined with human remains, piled to the vault overhead, in the fashion of the great catacombs of Paris. Three sides of this interior crypt were still ornamented in this manner. From the fourth the bones had been thrown down, and lay promiscuously upon the earth, forming at one point a mound of some size. Within the wall thus exposed by the displacing of the bones, we perceived a still interior recess, in depth about four feet, in width three, in height six or seven. It seemed to have been constructed for no especial use within itself, but formed merely the interval between two of the colossal supports of the roof of the catacombs, and was backed by one of their circumscribing walls of solid granite.

It was in vain that Fortunato, uplifting his dull torch, endeavored to pry into the depth of the recess. Its termination the feeble light did not enable us to see.

"Proceed," I said; "herein is the Amontillado. As for Luchesi — "

"He is an ignoramus," interrupted my friend, as he stepped unsteadily forward, while I followed immediately at his heels. In an instant he had reached the extremity of the niche, and finding his progress arrested by the rock, stood stupidly bewildered. A moment more and I had fettered[25] him to the granite. In its surface were two iron staples, distant from each other about two feet, horizontally. From one of these depended a short chain, from the other a padlock. Throwing the links about his waist, it was but the work of a few seconds to secure it. He was too much astounded to resist. Withdrawing the key, I stepped back from the recess.

"Pass your hand," I said, "over the wall; you cannot help feeling the nitre. Indeed it is *very* damp. Once more let me *implore* you to return. No? Then I must positively leave you. But I must first render you all the little attentions in my power."

"The Amontillado!" ejaculated my friend, not yet recovered from his astonishment.

"True," I replied; "the Amontillado."

As I said these words I busied myself among the pile of bones of which I have before spoken. Throwing them aside, I soon uncovered a quantity of building stone and mortar. With these materials and with the aid of my trowel, I began vigorously to wall up the entrance of the niche.

I had scarcely laid the first tier of the masonry when I discovered that the intoxication of Fortunato had in a great measure worn off. The earliest indication I had of this was a low moaning cry from the depth of the recess. It was *not* the cry of a drunken man. There was then a long and obstinate silence. I laid the second tier, and the third, and the fourth; and then I heard the furious vibrations of the chain. The noise lasted for several minutes, during which, that I might hearken to it with the more satisfaction, I ceased my labors and sat down upon the bones. When at last the clanking subsided, I resumed the trowel, and finished without interruption the fifth, the sixth, and the seventh tier. The wall was now nearly upon a level with my breast. I again paused, and holding the flambeaux over the masonwork, threw a few feeble rays upon the figure within.

A succession of loud and shrill screams, bursting suddenly from the throat of the chained form, seemed to thrust me violently back. For a brief moment I hesitated — I trembled. Unsheathing my rapier,[26] I began to grope with it about the recess; but the thought of an instant reassured me. I placed my hand upon the solid fabric of the catacombs, and felt satisfied. I reapproached the wall. I replied to the yells of him who clamored. I reechoed — I aided — I surpassed them in volume and in strength. I did this, and the clamorer grew still.

It was now midnight, and my task was drawing to a close. I had completed the eighth, the ninth, and the tenth tier. I had finished a portion of the last and the eleventh; there remained but a single stone to be fitted and plastered in. I struggled with its weight; I placed it partially in its destined position. But now there came from out the niche a low laugh that erected the hairs upon my head. It was succeeded by a sad voice, which I had difficulty in recognizing as that of the noble Fortunato. It said —

"Ha! ha! ha! — he! he! — a very good joke indeed — an excellent jest. We will have many a rich laugh about it at the palazzo — he! he! he! — over our wine — he! he! he!"

"The Amontillado!" I said.

"He! he! he! — He! he! he! — yes, the Amontillado. But is it not getting late? Will not they be awaiting us at the palazzo, the Lady Fortunato and the rest? Let us be gone."

"Yes," I said, "let us be gone."

*"For the love of God, Montresor!"*

"Yes," I said, "for the love of God!"

But to these words I hearkened in vain for a reply. I grew impatient. I called aloud:

"Fortunato!"

No answer. I called again:

"Fortunato!"

No answer still. I thrust a torch through the remaining aperture[27] and let it fall within. There came forth in return only a jingling of the bells. My heart grew sick — on account of the dampness of the catacombs. I hastened to make an end of my labor. I forced the last stone into its position; I plastered it up. Against the new masonry I re-erected the old rampart of bones. For half of a century no mortal has disturbed them.

*In pace requiescat!*[28]

[1] **impunity:** freedom from punishment

[2] **unredressed:** not set right

[3] **retribution:** something given in response to something done, especially punishment

[4] **immolation:** execution as a sacrificial victim

[5] **connoisseurship:** expert knowledge

[6] **virtuoso:** one who is skilled in or has an appreciation for the fine arts

[7] **carnival:** season or festival of merrymaking before Lent

[8] **motley:** multi-colored costume worn by a clown or fool

[9] **pipe:** large cask

[10] **Amontillado:** a type of wine

[11] **nitre:** salt deposits

[12] **roquelaure:** short cloak

[13] **absconded:** left quickly and secretly; fled

[14] **flambeaux:** torches

[15] **catacombs:** underground burial place that has passages with hollowed places in the sides for graves

[16] **orbs:** eyes

[17] **rheum:** a watery discharge

[18] **arms:** coat of arms; family insignia

[19] **A huge . . . heel:** The Montresor coat of arms shows a huge golden foot, in a blue field, crushing a serpent whose teeth are sunk into the heel.

[20] *Nemo me impune lacessit:* No one provokes me with impunity.

[21] **puncheon:** cask holding up to 120 gallons

[22] **masons:** a secret fraternal society or brotherhood. The word *mason* also means "bricklayer."

[23] **trowel:** a small hand tool used for spreading cement or plaster

[24] **crypt:** underground room or vault generally used as a burial place

[25] **fettered:** chained

[26] **rapier:** sword with a double-edged blade

[27] **aperture:** opening

[28] *In pace requiescat:* May he rest in peace.

## A CLOSER LOOK

*1. Explain Montresor's family motto. How does it relate to his pursuit of revenge?*

*2. What is Fortunato's weak point? How does Montresor make use of that weak point to take his revenge?*

*3. Why is it ironic that Fortunato is wearing a fool's costume? Why is the last line of the story ironic?*

*4. The term* **foreshadowing** *refers to clues in a story that hint at events to come. Poe uses foreshadowing in this story when he has Montresor show his trowel to Fortunato. What later event does the trowel foreshadow?*

*5. According to Poe, the purpose of a story is to arouse in the reader a single powerful emotion. In "The Cask of Amontillado," that emotion is horror, and Poe includes nothing that might distract us from that feeling. Notice, for example, that he never tells us how Fortunato injured and insulted Montresor. Suppose Poe had included this information. What questions might it raise in our minds? What feelings might it arouse in us? Why would such questions and feelings distract us from the single strong emotion Poe wants us to feel?*

• When the Czar of Russia freed the serfs[1] (peasants) in 1861, they were no longer forced to work on their owners' estates. But poverty was so widespread that some peasants, like Vanka's[2] mother and grandfather, were able to survive only by returning to work on the estates of their former owners, the Russian nobility. Other peasants, like Vanka himself, had to look for jobs in the cities. In this story, Vanka has gone to Moscow to become an apprentice to a shoemaker. As an apprentice, he must do any task his master demands in return for room, board, and regular instruction. If he succeeds in learning a trade, Vanka will escape the hardships of peasant life. But first, he must survive his apprenticeship.

# Anton Chekhov

# VANKA

NINE-YEAR-OLD VANKA ZHUKOV, WHO WAS apprenticed three months ago to the shoemaker Alyakhin, did not go to bed on Christmas Eve. He waited till the master and mistress and the more senior apprentices had gone to the early service, and then he took a bottle of ink and a pen with a rusty nib from his master's cupboard, and began to write on a crumpled sheet of paper spread out in front of him. Before tracing the shape of the first letter, he looked several times fearfully in the direction of the doors and windows, and then he gazed up at the dark icon,[3] flanked on either side by shelves filled with cobbler's lasts,[4] and then he heaved a broken sigh. With the paper spread over the bench, Vanka knelt on the floor beside it.

"Dear Grandfather Konstantin Makarich," he wrote. "I am writing a letter to you. I wish you a Merry Christmas and all good things from the Lord God. I have no father and mother, and you are all I have left."

Vanka raised his eyes to the dark windowpane, on which there gleamed the reflection of a candle flame, and in his vivid imagination he saw his grandfather Konstantin Makarich standing there. His grandfather was a night watchman on the estate of some gentlefolk named Zhivaryov, a small, thin, unusually lively and nimble old man of about sixty-five, his face always crinkling with laughter, and his eyes bleary from drink. In the daytime the old man slept in the servants' kitchen or cracked jokes with the cooks. At night, wrapped in an ample sheepskin coat, he made the rounds of the estate, shaking his clapper.[5] Two dogs followed him with drooping heads — one was the old female Brownie, the other was a male called Eel because of his black coat and long weasely body. Eel always seemed to be extraordinarily respectful and endearing, gazing with the same fond eyes on friends and strangers alike; yet no one trusted him. His deference[6] and humility concealed a most cunning malice.[7] No one knew better how to creep stealthily behind someone and take a nip at his leg, or how to crawl into the icehouse, or how to scamper off with a peasant's chicken. More than once they just about broke his hind legs, twice a noose was put round his neck, and every week he was beaten until he was only half alive, yet he always managed to survive.

At this very moment Grandfather was probably standing by the gates, screwing up his eyes at the bright red windows of the village church, stamping about in his felt boots and cracking jokes with the servants. His clapper hung from his belt. He would be throwing out his arms and then hugging himself against the cold, and, hiccupping as old men do, he would be pinching one of the servant girls or one of the cooks.

"What about a pinch of snuff, eh?" he would say, holding out his snuffbox.

Then the women would take a pinch and sneeze, and the old man would be overcome with indescribable ecstasies, laughing joyously and exclaiming: "Fine for frozen noses, eh!"

The dogs, too, were given snuff. Brownie would sneeze, shake her head, and walk away looking offended, while Eel, too polite to sneeze, only wagged his tail. The weather was glorious. The air was still, transparently clear, and fresh. The night was very dark, but the whole white-roofed village, with its snowdrifts and trees silvered with hoarfrost[8] and smoke streaming from the chimneys, could be seen clearly. The heavens were sprinkled with gay, glinting stars, and the Milky Way stood out as clearly as if it had been washed and scrubbed with snow for the holidays.

Vanka sighed, dipped his pen in the ink, and went on writing: "Yesterday I was given a thrashing. The master dragged me by the hair into the yard and gave me a beating with a stirrup strap because when I was rocking the baby in the cradle, I fell asleep. And then last week the mistress ordered me to gut a herring, and because I began with the tail, she took the head of the herring and rubbed it all over my face. The other apprentices made fun of me, sent me to the tavern for vodka, and made me steal the master's cucumbers for them, and then the master beat me with the first thing that came to hand. And there's nothing to eat. In the morning they give me bread, there is porridge for dinner, and in the evening only bread again. They never give me tea or cabbage soup — they gobble it all up themselves. They make me sleep in the passageway, and when their baby cries, I don't get any sleep at all because I have to rock the cradle. Dear Grandfather, please for God's sake take me away from here, take me to the village, it's more than I can bear. . . . I kneel down before you. I'll pray to God to keep you forever, but take me away from here, or I shall die."

Vanka grimaced, rubbed his eyes with his black fists, and sobbed.

"I'll grind your snuff for you," he went on. "I will pray to God to keep you, and if I ever do anything wrong, you can flog me all you like. If you think there's no place for me, then I'll ask the manager for Christ's sake to let me clean boots or take Fedya's place as a shepherd boy. Dear Grandfather, it's more than I can bear, it will be the death of me. I thought of running away to the village, but I haven't any boots, and I am afraid of the ice. If you'll do this for me, I'll feed you when I grow up, and won't let anyone harm you, and when you die, I'll pray for the repose[9] of your soul, just like I do for my mother.

"Moscow is such a big city. There are so many houses belonging to the gentry,[10] so many horses, but no sheep anywhere, and the dogs aren't vicious. The boys don't go about with the Star of Christmas, and they don't let you sing in the choir, and once I saw fishhooks in the shop window with the fishing lines for every kind of fish, very fine ones, even one hook which would hold a skate fish weighing forty pounds. I've seen shops selling guns which are just like the master's at home, and each one must cost a hundred rubles.[11] In the butcher shops they have woodcocks and partridges and hares, but the people in the shop won't tell you where they were shot.

"Dear Grandfather, when they put up the Christmas tree at the big house, please take down a golden walnut for me and hide it in the green chest. Ask the young mistress, Olga Ignatyevna, and say it is for Vanka."

Vanka heaved a convulsive sigh, and once more he gazed in the

direction of the window. He remembered it was Grandfather who always went to the forest to cut down a Christmas tree for the gentry, taking his grandson with him. They had a wonderful time together. Grandfather chuckled, the frost crackled, and Vanka, not to be outdone, clucked away cheerfully. Before chopping down the fir tree, Grandfather would smoke a pipe, take a long pinch of snuff, and make fun of Vanka, who was shivering in the cold. The young fir trees, garlanded with hoarfrost, stood perfectly still, waiting to see which of them would die. . . . Suddenly out of nowhere a hare came springing across the snowdrifts, quick as an arrow, and Grandfather would be unable to prevent himself from shouting: "Hold him! Hold him! Hold that bobtailed devil, eh!"

When the tree had been chopped down, Grandfather would drag it to the big house and they would start decorating it. The young mistress, Olga Ignatyevna, Vanka's favorite, was the busiest of all. While Vanka's mother, Pelageya, was alive, serving as a chamber-maid, Olga Ignatyevna used to stuff him with sugar candy, and it amused her to teach him to read and write, to count up to a hundred, and even to dance the quadrille.[12] But when Pelageya died, they relegated the orphan Vanka to the servants' kitchen to be with his grandfather, and from there he went to Moscow to the shoemaker Alyakhin. . . .

"Come to me, dear Grandfather," Vanka went on. "I beseech[13] you for Christ's sake, take me away from here! Have pity on me, a poor orphan, they are always beating me, and I am terribly hungry, and so miserable I can't tell you, and I'm always crying. The other day the master hit me on the head with a last, and I fell down and thought I would never get up again. It's worse than a dog's life, and so miserable. I send greetings to Alyona, to one-eyed Yegor, and to the coachman, and don't give my harmonica away. I re-main your grandson Ivan Zhukov, dear Grandfather, and come soon!"

Vanka twice folded the sheet of paper and then he put it in an envelope bought the previous day for a kopeck.[14] He reflected for a while, dipped the pen in ink, and wrote the address: To Grandfa-ther in the Village. Then he scratched his head and thought for a while, and added the words: Konstantin Makarich. Pleased because no one had interrupted him when he was writing, he threw on his cap, and without troubling to put on a coat, he ran out into the street.

When he had talked to the clerks in the butcher shop the pre-vious day, they had told him that letters were dropped in boxes, and from these boxes they were carried all over the world on mail coaches drawn by three horses and driven by drunken drivers, while the bells jingled. Vanka ran to the nearest mailbox and thrust his precious letter into the slot.

An hour later, lulled by sweetest hopes, he was fast asleep. He dreamed of a stove. His grandfather was sitting on the stove, bare feet dangling down, while he read the letter aloud to the cooks. Eel was walking round the stove, wagging his tail.

[1] **serfs:** members of a feudal class who are obliged to work the land belonging to their masters
[2] **Vanka:** nickname for Ivan (John). In English, he would be called Johnny.
[3] **icon:** picture of a religious figure or saint, usually painted on wood
[4] **cobbler's lasts:** wooden forms on which leather is shaped into shoes
[5] **clapper:** hammerlike object inside a bell
[6] **deference:** courteous respect
[7] **malice:** ill will; spite
[8] **hoarfrost:** frost
[9] **repose:** peace; condition of being at rest
[10] **gentry:** upper or ruling class
[11] **ruble:** Russian unit of money
[12] **quadrille:** a square dance performed by four couples
[13] **beseech:** beg
[14] **kopeck:** 100 kopecks make one ruble

## A CLOSER LOOK

*1. Apprentices like Vanka were legally bound to perform any service their masters demanded for a period of years, usually seven. Some masters treated their apprentices as students, while others treated them more like slaves. What kind of master does Vanka have? Support your answer with evidence from the story.*

*2. Telling the story from a child's point of view gives the author a chance to remind us of our kinship with other forms of life. Vanka sees "human" qualities in animals and even in plants. Describe the "personality" of the dog Eel. Give evidence from the story to support your statements.*

*3. What thought or emotion does Vanka give to the fir trees in the woods where he and Grandfather go to find a Christmas tree?*

*4. Look at the address Vanka wrote on the letter to his grandfather. Is it likely that the letter will reach his grandfather? Why or why not?*

● Every day for twenty years, the engineer had slowed his train down so he could wave to the woman and her daughter. And every day for twenty years, the two women had waved back. This exchange had given the engineer the greatest and most enduring pleasure of his life. Now, on the day of his retirement, he is paying them a surprise visit.

## Thomas Wolfe

# THE FAR AND THE NEAR

ON THE OUTSKIRTS OF A LITTLE TOWN UPON A rise of land that swept back from the railway there was a tidy little cottage of white boards, trimmed vividly with green blinds. To one side of the house there was a garden neatly patterned with plots of growing vegetables, and an arbor for the grapes which ripened late in August. Before the house there were three mighty oaks which sheltered it in their clean and massive shade in summer, and to the other side there was a border of gay flowers. The whole place had an air of tidiness, thrift, and modest comfort.

Every day, a few minutes after two o'clock in the afternoon, the limited express between two cities passed this spot. At that moment the great train, having halted for a breathing-space at the town nearby, was beginning to lengthen evenly into its stroke, but it had not yet reached the full drive of its terrific speed. It swung into view deliberately, swept past with a powerful swaying motion of the engine, a low smooth rumble of its heavy cars upon pressed steel, and then it vanished in the cut. For a moment the progress of the engine could be marked by heavy bellowing puffs of smoke that burst at spaced intervals above the edges of the meadow grass, and finally nothing could be heard but the solid clacking tempo of the wheels receding into the drowsy stillness of the afternoon.

Every day for more than twenty years, as the train had approached this house, the engineer had blown on the whistle, and every day, as soon as she heard this signal, a woman had appeared on the back porch of the little house and waved to him. At first she had a small child clinging to her skirts, and now this child had

82

grown to full womanhood, and every day she, too, came with her mother to the porch and waved.

The engineer had grown old and gray in service. He had driven his great train, loaded with its weight of lives, across the land ten thousand times. His own children had grown up and married, and four times he had seen before him on the tracks the ghastly dot of tragedy converging[1] like a cannon ball to its eclipse of horror at the boiler head — a light spring wagon filled with children, with its clustered row of small stunned faces; a cheap automobile stalled upon the tracks, set with the wooden figures of people paralyzed with fear; a battered hobo walking by the rail, too deaf and old to hear the whistle's warning; and a form flung past his window with a scream — all this the man had seen and known. He had known all the grief, the joy, the peril and the labor such a man could know; he had grown seamed and weathered in his loyal service, and now, schooled by the qualities of faith and courage and humbleness that attended his labor, he had grown old, and had the grandeur and the wisdom these men have.

But no matter what peril or tragedy he had known, the vision of the little house and the women waving to him with a brave free motion of the arm had become fixed in the mind of the engineer as something beautiful and enduring, something beyond all change and ruin, and something that would always be the same, no matter what mishap, grief or error might break the iron schedule of his days.

The sight of the little house and of these two women gave him the most extraordinary happiness he had ever known. He had seen them in a thousand lights, a hundred weathers. He had seen them through the harsh bare light of wintry gray across the brown and frosted stubble of the earth, and he had seen them again in the green luring sorcery of April.

He felt for them and for the little house in which they lived such tenderness as a man might feel for his own children, and at length the picture of their lives was carved so sharply in his heart that he

felt that he knew their lives completely, to every hour and moment of the day, and he resolved that one day, when his years of service should be ended, he would go and find these people and speak at last with them whose lives had been so wrought into his own.

That day came. At last the engineer stepped from a train onto the station platform of the town where these two women lived. His years upon the rail had ended. He was a pensioned servant of his company, with no more work to do. The engineer walked slowly through the station and out into the streets of the town. Everything was as strange to him as if he had never seen this town before. As he walked on, his sense of bewilderment and confusion grew. Could this be the town he had passed ten thousand times? Were these the same houses he had seen so often from the high windows of his cab? It was all as unfamiliar, as disquieting as a city in a dream, and the perplexity[2] of his spirit increased as he went on.

Presently the houses thinned into the straggling outposts of the town, and the street faded into a country road — the one on which the women lived. And the man plodded on slowly in the heat and dust. At length he stood before the house he sought. He knew at once that he had found the proper place. He saw the lordly oaks before the house, the flower beds, the garden and the arbor, and farther off, the glint of rails.

Yes, this was the house he sought, the place he had passed so many times, the destination he had longed for with such happiness. But now that he had found it, now that he was here, why did his hand falter on the gate; why had the town, the road, the earth, the very entrance to this place he loved turned unfamiliar as the landscape of some ugly dream? Why did he now feel this sense of confusion, doubt and hopelessness?

At length he entered by the gate, walked slowly up the path and in a moment more had mounted three short steps that led up to the porch, and was knocking at the door. Presently he heard steps in the hall, the door was opened, and a woman stood facing him.

And instantly, with a sense of bitter loss and grief, he was sorry he had come. He knew at once that the woman who stood there looking at him with a mistrustful eye was the same woman who had waved to him so many thousand times. But her face was harsh and pinched and meager;[3] the flesh sagged wearily in sallow folds, and the small eyes peered at him with timid suspicion and uneasy doubt. All the brave freedom, the warmth and the affection that he had read into her gesture, vanished in the moment that he saw her and heard her unfriendly tongue.

And now his own voice sounded unreal and ghastly to him as he tried to explain his presence, to tell her who he was and the reason he had come. But he faltered on, fighting stubbornly against the horror of regret, confusion, disbelief that surged up in his spirit, drowning all his former joy and making his act of hope and tenderness seem shameful to him.

At length the woman invited him almost unwillingly into the house, and called her daughter in a harsh shrill voice. Then, for a brief agony of time, the man sat in an ugly little parlor, and he tried to talk while the two women stared at him with a dull, bewildered hostility, a sullen, timorous[4] restraint.

And finally, stammering a crude farewell, he departed. He walked away down the path and then along the road toward town, and suddenly he knew that he was an old man. His heart, which had been brave and confident when it looked along the familiar vista of the rails, was now sick with doubt and horror as it saw the strange and unsuspected visage[5] of an earth which had always been within a stone's throw of him, and which he had never seen or known. And he knew that all the magic of that bright lost way, the vista of that shining line, the imagined corner of that small good universe of hope's desire, was gone forever, could never be got back again.

[1] **converging:** coming together; moving toward a common point
[2] **perplexity:** confusion; bewilderment
[3] **meager:** thin
[4] **timorous:** fearful
[5] **visage:** appearance; face

## A CLOSER LOOK

*1. What did the sight of the little house and the women waving to him mean to the engineer? Compare his fantasy to the reality. Do you think he had only been seeing what he wanted to see? Or had the people and the place really changed? Explain.*

*2. Why do you suppose the woman and her daughter waved to the engineer every day for more than twenty years?*

*3. Before he entered the house, the engineer realized it would be a mistake to talk to the women. What made him realize this? He might have gone away. Why do you think he didn't?*

• Sixty-year-old Abel Delahanty lives alone in a stone cottage next to a creek that empties into the great Hudson River. His great joy is living amid the beauty of nature. His greatest joy is the coming of the geese in the spring. But Abel has a sadness, too, a longing for something that he feels but can't identify.

# Edmund Gilligan

# A WILD GOOSE FALLS

**A**N APRIL SNOW LAY SCATTERED AND MELTING on the banks of Ram's Horn Creek, where Abel Delahanty idly paddled his duckboat on an ebbing tide. Vivid against frost-cracked stems of winter, the fresh stalks cast their shadows on traces of snow. At times, while he floated down the winding passage to the Hudson River, the wind whirled tiny spouts of snow crystals across his hands. The crystals vanished at once in the warmth of his seamed, scarred hands — great, dark hands that never changed in color because their labor never changed. Aloft and farther downstream rare music sounded and gentled his mouth to a serene smile. "Ah, it's you, is it?"

On the bare crown of a dead ash tree a hermit thrush sang its intricate, sweet-toned phrases. The bird held its head so clear against the sky that Abel could see its brown, mottled[1] throat pulsing. When he glided under the tree, his paddle at ease, he heard the bird's mate uttering her response in the quiet cedars yonder.

Around Long Bend, the cat-o'-nine-tails[2] took the place of wild rice, and red-winged blackbirds perched on the cat-o'-nine-tails spikes and called gaily across the water. Where the bend straightened toward the river, he smiled in a fresh pleasure, for here he saw the first flower of spring, an arbutus — one white blossom, one nearly pink — in a glowing array upon a rift of snow.

The marsh grew louder with springtime music — murmur of the tide against fallen stalk, rustle of first leaves of hazel trees and alders. Where the lagoons lay quiet in the sun, he heard the chatter of wood ducks at their housekeeping in the box nests he had put up for them. He then heard chords of other, wilder music far away.

# A WILD GOOSE FALLS

The better to listen, he laid his paddle across his knees and gazed into the eastward sky. For most of his sixty years he had eagerly awaited those wilderness bugle notes aloft, in springtime and in autumn, yet his joy on first hearing them after a winter's silence had never waned. The cry of geese meant more to him than all other music. The falling tide tugged so briskly at his boat that a gurgling sound marred the silence. He laid hold of an alder bough and ran his boat into a shoal of lily pads. There the sunlight fell freely upon him. He took off his cap to enjoy the warmth, to let it soothe his bony, wind-stained cheeks. The wind stirred his disorderly thatch of black hair, streaked by gray where it lay down the nape of his neck.

He scanned the southern sky. A party of mallard ducks burst out of the reeds in such a clatter of wings and voices that for a time he could hear no hint of the approaching music. Soon it rang delicately clear, this time closer. At last, a wedge[3] of wild geese — thirty birds and more — came winging in toward the river. He could tell that they were weary after a night of flying against the winds. Their wings beat heavily. They flew through such a dazzle of sunlight that he could see milder gleams piercing their pinions[4] in the outward beats. Even while he watched, he made out another sign of weariness. Their leader, in the van[5] to break a passage and steer their immemorial[6] course, cried out a signal, asking for relief from that harsh duty. The pattern broke to let another goose take the lead. The wedge formed again and flew on toward Abel's place. "And now you are here!"

Once again he smiled in pleasure at their beauty; and then, his heart roused by their weariness, he cupped his hands and called to them, "Aroink! Aroink!" He knew that at times, especially after a long flight in darkness, they became confused and might pass over a resting place, a shelter such as the great marsh provided.

The geese were now directly overhead. They had heard his greeting call. The leader veered away and rose in a turn toward the marsh. The wedge swung lower. The first birds set their wings for a descent. At that moment, Abel heard a shout on the riverbank above the mouth of the creek. He believed it to be a cry of pleasure from another watcher. He was about to call the geese again when a rifle shot cracked in that direction. This angered him. He flinched at the echo. He didn't think a true rifleman would attempt such a shot. Yet he gazed anxiously at the geese.

They had heard the shot. In silence they began to climb in

shorter, brisker beats to their first course for the river. Abruptly the V pattern broke again. Their cries rang piteously aloft, cries of fear and bafflement. A bird at the end of the wedge soared downward in a faltering manner. Others turned sharply after it and soared beneath it. Such a confused jabbering began up there that Abel knew something had gone wrong among the yearling birds to which the easier flight positions in the rear were assigned. When that faltering bird set its wings and slanted down, he understood what had happened. The careless rifle shot, fired for no reason at all, had struck that bird.

The wounded bird flashed out of sight beyond the willows at the river's edge, where their fresh leaves created a mild, green haze.

Bitterly Abel blamed himself for his call to the geese. He had lured them out of their course. Because of his action, one goose lay dying on the river. The image hurt him. Long, long ago he had ceased to hunt those birds because he did not care to interfere at all with their lives, their hard passages to the bays of Canada or the bays of Virginia. Now he had unwittingly[7] hurt one of them, bound north to their ancestral breeding grounds, to the mate, the nest, eggs, and beloved gosling[8]-to-be.

His sorrow became worse because he believed there was nothing he could do except to resolve that he would never call geese again. Even so, he did not resist the impulse of his heart that forced him to take up his paddle and send his boat gliding swiftly around the last bend. In that passage toward the river all his joy in the return of spring — the buds of his thousand apple trees, the thrush song and arbutus's gleam — changed, not exactly to sadness but to a melancholy strain, as if he had just learned, far too late, a lesson he couldn't quite comprehend. Often before, he had heard an inward voice hinting of a lack, a hidden, tender desire. It had never taken a true form; and it did not now, even in this keen access[9] of its strength.

A vessel beyond the willows bayed a signal. Gliding in much beauty, its azure hull matching the sky and its white bridge matching the clouds, a Swedish freighter bound for the port of Albany showed itself in the openings of the forest. Flying low over its wake, a number of gulls vaulted upward. At first Abel believed the gulls were following the vessel in a search for food. They were not. They were answering signals from other gulls that screamed in a place hidden from him by reeds.

Abel knew that gulls prefer to keep silent. Their endless flying creates endless hunger. Except for early-morning crankiness, when famine is at its worst among them, they search in silence, heads down, eyes glaringly intent. Nothing eatable escapes their vision. So scanty is their fare that they must examine every floating object, even a bit of odd-colored cloth. He had often seen them at the moment of discovery when the hope of meat excited them to shrieks of exultation. He had seen them in cruel actions many a time, even in his orchard, where they soared hawklike, watching for a rabbit that had met disaster. The screams he now heard were just such blares of exultation.

His boat struck into the river. He steered toward a sandbar. There he saw the gulls that had been concealed. They were coursing downstream, rising in silent, frantic curves, then swooping. It was in the swoop that they shrieked. And they rose and fell in a pattern of eight or nine birds, one following the other, and the first curving hastily back to swoop and scream again, "What are you up to now?"

Abel thought they had caught sight of a crippled striped bass or, possibly, an injured duckling, lost from a brood of native mallards. He had seen such attacks by them and had counted it in the ways of nature, ways to be accepted. Nevertheless, that first impulse had not entirely died in his heart. At the next cry — not from a gull — his impulse became something stronger: a call to action. He had never heard such a cry before. He could tell only that neither a gull nor a duckling had uttered it.

At the next stroke of his paddle and after a long glide forward he saw what was crying so strangely — a young goose, a gander[10] thrusting violently forward, unable to rise because its wings beat too weakly. When its gray breast surged up from the ripple, a spurt of blood glittered. A gull swooped and struck at the gander's head. The gander shrank and tried to dive. He could not. Violent blows of his wings baffled the next attack. The second attacker swept off, and a third came in its turn, its beak closed to stab. Again the gander thrust his head into the poor protection of the water. The gulls were trying to drown the gander. When he lifted his head to breathe, a gull struck him between the eyes. Blood appeared on the gander's white cheek.

The gander had seen the reeds along the shore. He kept trying to reach them. Repeated blows hurt him so much that he could not stay on that course. He tried to fly. His wings struck spray around him. This effort cost him so much strength that he folded his wings and lay shuddering on the tide, his beak under water. Two gulls alighted near him and swam toward his head. Abel thrust his paddle deep and drove his boat between the gulls and the gander. He lifted the wounded bird into the boat. The gulls flew silently away.

During the passage up the creek the gander lay on its side. It seemed lifeless. Blood seeped out of its breast feathers on the right side. Abel knew this wound had been made by the rifle bullet. He went ashore where the creek flowed out of his pond. He wrapped the gander in a strip of soft canvas and trudged up the lane to his stone cottage, where he had fended for himself many a long year. He carried the gander into his workshop, where he mended his tools and tied trout flies on winter evenings. He switched on the strong lamp of his fly-tying vise[11] and parted the feathers that lay soggy over the wound. It was then that he found the other wound, where the bullet had passed through the gander's back. When he began cutting away the dark feathers of the back, the gander feebly struck with his beak.

"Good for you, gander! Where there's such a life, there's hope."

He stopped both wounds with adhesive tape and placed the bird in a box of straw near the coal stove of his kitchen. After watching a time, Abel saw that the gander couldn't keep its head up. He nailed in a wooden support and bound the gander to it, making sure it could breathe. In a little while the gander made a croaking sound and wearily clacked his beak.

"Now if you live the night, friend, I'll do more for you if I can."

During the night the gander repeated his croaking call so loudly that Abel came into the kitchen. At the touch of his hand, the gander beat his wings frantically. This show of strength encouraged Abel so much that he removed the support. In doing this he had to touch the gander. It began a low clucking and lay so quietly in the straw that Abel perceived the bird had lost all fear of him. At daybreak, when he made his porridge of oatmeal, he mixed some with milk and tried to spoon it into the gander's gullet. This didn't work well, but the bird didn't flinch.

The next day, when Abel returned from the first spraying of his orchard, he found the gander out of the nest. It hadn't gone far. That night the gander willingly thrust its bill into a deep dish of porridge and fed in desperate awkwardness.

On Sunday Abel carried the gander to the shore of his pond and put it down on the sunlit grass, close enough to the water so that the gander could go in if it wished to do so. There were two tenants of the pond, a pair of white barnyard ducks, one called Henry and the other Alice. Their only duty was to look pretty. They spoke amiably to the gander and made no objection at all when he joined them at their dish of mash. Abel left the three together. When he came back, he found the gander in the water, not swimming, just floating near the shore.

In the following days the gander became quite friendly with the ducks, despite the incredulous stares that they often turned upon him. He began to swim farther and farther after them. Yet he considered Abel his best friend. At nightfall, when Abel stood by the door and clapped his hands, the gander came out of the reeds and took its place in the kitchen nest.

Before another week had passed, the gander tried its wings. To the ducks, far too plump ever to manage more than a stately waddle, his first flight seemed an astonishing feat. When he rose they looked, not at him, but at each other. Abel watched the gander rise higher and higher. Once above the elms, the gander uttered an exulting cry. He flew well, and his wounds had healed. Yet Abel feared that the gander couldn't go north by itself, that it might come to worse harm. In its flight the gander displayed such beauty that Abel wished it never to leave him. He struck his hands together and shouted. At once the gander set its wings and slanted down to the pond.

Despite his pleasure in the gander's company, Abel took no long time to understand that, once again, he was interfering with the life of a creature apart from him and his ways. This idea came in the middle of a rainy night when a flight of geese on the way north flew so close to his rooftree that their shouting awakened him. Their cries had disturbed the gander, too. He began that curious croaking. Twice he beat his wings loudly in his nest.

Before the gander began its next flight over the pond, it stayed awhile under the lilac boughs, where the first clusters were blooming. Its head lowered, it appeared to be brooding. At times it thrust its beak into the repaired feathers of its breast. When the ducks paddled out of the reeds and quacked their greetings, the gander rose into the wind. This flight carried it higher than ever before, so high, indeed, that Abel feared it might never return to him. Aloft the gander cried plaintively.

It rode the wind toward the marsh and slowly veered into a circling passage over the rows of apple trees, all in white bloom.

Abel knew the purpose of such flights when they were made in the wilderness. They were made to fix in the bird's memory an image of the birthplace, the bays around it, and the islands. Thus the landmarks were learned. By following their mothers in the first water journeys, then in the short flights, they learned to go farther and farther from their nests and to return at night. Flying a greater distance each day, the geese became familiar with the Canadian marshes. Before the migrations[12] began, they had flown a hundred miles away and had returned. When gales and ice forced them into the first stages of migration, they added new memories to their memories of the earlier waters.

Abel made up his mind then and there not to summon the gander down. So many geese were coming into the marsh, day and night, that he convinced himself, not very easily, that his friend would find company for the migration. He went to bed. At daybreak he found the gander waiting on the doorstep.

"This won't do, gander. You must go north with the others."

So, about noontime, he called the gander, fed him well, and took him in his arms to the duckboat. He paddled down Ram's Horn Creek, the gander's head resting quietly on the gunwale[13] forward. At the river's edge, under willows beginning to bend under new leaves, Abel listened. He heard a grouse drumming and a pheasant crowing beyond the willows. Wood ducks flashed away.

Abel drove his boat into a high stand of rice on the riverbank. There, above the rustling of a flood tide, he heard geese at their gossip in the reeds. Three geese glided out. Others followed, until there were about forty floating idly about.

"Now, gander, here be your true friends. You go to them. Do you hear? Good-bye and good luck — and I'm sorry I kind of delayed things for you."

He placed the gander in the water. It left the reeds and swam out. The tide carried it toward the flock. The flock came slowly on — one with its head high and eyes alert. They greeted the newcomer with low, chuckling cries.

When the gander had entered the flock, Abel struck the water flatly with his paddle. In a thrash of wings, all the birds flew off and down the river. They mounted directly toward the sun. For a time Abel saw nothing because the light dazzled his eyes. Soon, out of the sun, a newly formed wedge flew northward. He heard their first cries in various tones. After that the steady "Aroink! Aroink!" began, the trumpet cries of the elder birds rallying all to the thousands of miles yet before them.

"Good-bye to you, gander. Good-bye."

Summer flushed across his lands. Fragrances of apple blossoms changed to fragrances of ripening fruit. With every passing day the labor in Abel's orchards increased. He hired men for the picking and worked on, making ready for the last of autumn. Soon boxes began to pile up in his barns; and the leaves of the elms changed to yellow and floated down.

In this time, especially at night when the work was well done, Abel used to take a turn along the edge of the pond and look up at the harvest moon, changing from red to gold over the river. He thought very often about his wild goose, his tamed wild goose gone wild again. He imagined the gander far over the Canadian border, perhaps in the marshes north of Saskatchewan. It seemed strange to him that the gander had come to have such a deep meaning, for he considered himself, by nature, not a lonely man. He had had a man's share of company in his time. Nevertheless, he couldn't stop the workings of a heart that sent his thought far up into the red moon, and beyond the Great Bear, and the Pole Star, and on into the vast spaces of wind and light where his companion had ventured with the migrating flock.

*Why should I think of him so much, eh? A man would think I'd done some lasting harm to him. Maybe I did so, in calling to them. But I didn't mean it so.*

He lay awake one night awhile longer than usual. He had taken half of his apples to market and had found a fair price for them. The other half he had put in storage to wait for a better price. Once he had figured out his books in his mind, he found his drowsy thought turning again to the lost gander. And by staying with his thought, by driving it along the starry routes of their flight, he struck upon a reason why, in his mind and heart, the wounded goose had such a meaning.

*It's because I love them so. Because they are brave and wise, and they know the ways of the eagle in the air, which the Scripture tells us we can't know.*

He considered the wild geese to be a mystery. That was it. Who could ever explain the melancholy, sweet influence their migrating chant had in the hearts of all men who listened? To him, and to all men, their ways were wonderful and strange, just as wonderful as were the flood tides and the ebb. What a wonder of creation that a moon, a quarter of a million miles away, could drive neap tides[14] so loudly through the rice and cat-o'-nine-tails. Abel had seen the moon more than once through a great telescope and had read the names of spaces called "seas" on the face of the moon. Those were tideless estuaries,[15] tideless creeks. The moon held no water and could not; yet, twice in a day — by a power no man had ever figured out — those empty lands raised the waters of earth, even to Ram's Horn Creek.

And, he told himself, the wild geese knew just as much about the moon as he did, if not more. Moons and tides were parts of their being. Indeed, they were creatures of the moon, were its partners. They liked to fly by the light of full moons because such moons showed the way. And they knew tides, too. Rafted on the river, they waited for high water until they could reach food without walking on muddy banks, from which they could not quickly rise in time of danger.

*Now I see. And I'll think no more of him, because by now he's learned all such things and wants me no more.*

His eyes closed. He had done a lot of thinking. He had worked it all out to his satisfaction. That was why he stirred angrily and murmured when, at the edge of sleep, a pang of longing coursed through his heart. Longing? No, he couldn't surely say that it was longing. A mystery had hold of him. He could not quiet himself until he let his heart have its way. This given, all his heart offered him was a memory of a migrating call, one to the other calling in the starlit sky where powerfully they flew, star by star, flighting away now from icebound waters and onward to estuaries that still obeyed the moon. He slept at last, his longing not understood, but put away in his secret heart where, forever and ever, other longings lay quiet, never moving him to tears again or to memories of tears once shed.

Winter winds sent the curled leaves soaring. Blackbirds met in tens of thousands over the marsh and, wings whirring louder than the scattering leaves, streamed away to the south. In the evenings, when winds blew off the river, Abel heard the high shrill chatter of teal and the wood ducks calling to their ducklings. He set out stores of grain for the chipmunks, who were still working hard, cheeks full, to fill their bins. At nightfall he went into the orchard and shook down apples from trees he kept apart for does and fawns, up from the marsh to taste early cider.

Employed at this duty, he heard the first flight of geese coming in from Canada. They were far across the river. Their rhythmic calls soon waned. Later in the night, while he read a book by the kitchen stove, he heard other geese. Louder and louder the calling sounded, and soon it, too, died away, leaving only an echo, not a true echo under his eaves, only an echo in his heart, endlessly repeated. The wind changed to the north, and a roaring like surf on an ice-strewn beach overwhelmed all other sounds. He had never noticed the north wind much. This time its tidelike music filled him with a kind of regret — and this surprised him. He carefully read over the page and closed the book to go to bed.

A lull came in the wind's blowing. It seemed to be dying down or hauling to the westward. When Abel opened his bedroom window, he heard again melancholy wailing of geese overhead, above the clouds close to the earth. As before, the music waned, and the night became silent; then, in keener accents, the music floated down to him. The calls were now coming from the north, and lower, much lower. It seemed clear to Abel that the geese were seeking the river and for some reason couldn't make sure of it. In a harsher, buglelike blare, the flock came over again, this time so far down that he peered out to see if he might not spy them against the stars.

Silence returned. But not for long. He had hardly closed his eyes when all the voices aloft sang out in an accent that seemed a

95

beseechment, many times repeated and always nearer. A gust of wind blew crackling out of the orchard and broke against the bare boughs of his elms in such a clatter that once again the goose cry fell away to nothing. Pity for the wayfarers rose in his heart. After daylong, nightlong beating against changing winds, their hearts and wings must now be weary. He wished they might find their way down. In a flood of fiery light the moon soared out of the clouds. Moonlight washed over the world to light the waters for the geese. They were silent.

At daybreak Abel began the easier chores of his winter months. He made his breakfast and went out into the yard to carry the mash to the ducks. To his surprise, Henry lay ashore, and near him stood Alice, plainly a little upset. They gazed at each other intently, bent their heads to new angles and looked smartly at each other sideways. They were in a witty mood, clucking and clacking.

Abel put down their pan. He walked to the pond. The cat-o'-nine-tails on the far side of the pond parted. A wild goose swam out, a handsome gander. Abel, not wishing to frighten the bird, stepped back a pace. The gander turned and entered the reeds. The bird's easy manner struck Abel quickly. He struck his hands together in the old signal. The gander came out, swam across the pond and came directly to Abel's feet.

"Is it you, gander? Really, is it you?"

Abel held out his hand. The gander laid his head on the outstretched fingers and made his curious croaking sound.

"Was it you, gander, flying over last night? Trying to come home?"

The gander stayed there a little longer. He repeated the sound, far down in his dark throat. After that he turned and swam back to the reeds, entering at exactly the same place. He began talking in there, a quick urgent note. Abel saw the beautiful wings and throat patch gleaming among the yellow stalks.

The reeds parted again and the gander appeared. He beat his wings lightly and swayed, rippling his image. There now came after him eight other geese, the first a lovely hen. The others were goslings, plump and strong in their flight feathers. To the gander's order they swam forward to the grass at Abel's feet.

"Why, you are welcome, gander and wife and goslings. Welcome home."

When the gander came ashore to be fondled again, there rose strongly in Abel's heart the same pang that had hurt him when the gander had departed. Even now, when all his anxiety had ended, he could not give a name to his heart's pain.

He bent down and whispered, "So you remembered me, gander?"

The moment he said the words, his heart cleared. He understood that all he had really wanted was to be remembered, to be remembered by somebody, something. Not to be forgotten.

1 **mottled:** having colored spots
2 **cat-o'-nine-tails:** tall reedlike marsh plants
3 **wedge:** formation of flying wild birds
4 **pinions:** end parts of birds' wings
5 **van:** first part of a procession
6 **immemorial:** extending back beyond the reach of memory or record
7 **unwittingly:** unknowingly; unintentionally
8 **gosling:** young goose
9 **access:** sudden and strong emotional outburst
10 **gander:** adult male goose
11 **vise:** tool with two jaws that clamp together to hold an object
12 **migration:** moving regularly from one region to another
13 **gunwale:** upper edge of a boat's side
14 **neap tides:** tides of medium range occuring at the first and third quarter of the moon
15 **estuaries:** narrow strips of water running from larger bodies of water into the land

## A CLOSER LOOK

*1. Why does Abel call the flock of geese? Why does he regret doing that?*

*2. Does Abel believe he has the right to change the ways of a wild creature? Find lines in the story that support your answer.*

*3. What is Abel's secret longing — the pang of longing he puts away in his secret heart? Is his longing ever answered? Explain.*

● "We hold these truths to be self-evident, that all men are created equal." What exactly did Thomas Jefferson mean when he wrote these words in the Declaration of Independence? Most people would agree that he meant all people are equal in the eyes of the law, and entitled to the same treatment in court. But suppose we took Jefferson's words one step further. Suppose we decided that all people must be equal — that is, exactly the same — in every way. And suppose we were able to accomplish this. Would the results be good or bad? Read the story and then decide.

# Kurt Vonnegut, Jr.

# HARRISON BERGERON

THE YEAR WAS 2081 A.D., AND EVERYBODY WAS finally equal. They weren't only equal before the law, they were equal every which way. Nobody was smarter than anybody else. Nobody was stronger or quicker. All this equality was due to the 211th, 212th, and 213th amendments to the Constitution, and to the unceasing vigilance[1] of agents of the United States Handicapper General.

Some things about living still weren't quite right, though. April, for instance, still drove people crazy by not being springtime. And it was in that clammy month that the H-G men took George and Hazel Bergeron's 14-year-old son Harrison away.

It was tragic, all right, but George and Hazel couldn't think about it very hard. Hazel had a perfectly average intelligence, which meant she couldn't think about anything except in short bursts. And George, whose intelligence was way above normal, had a little mental handicap radio in his ear.

He was required by law to wear it at all times and it was tuned to a government transmitter. Every 20 seconds or so, the transmitter would send out some sharp noise to keep George — and people like him — from taking unfair advantage of their brains.

George and Hazel were watching television. There were tears on Hazel's cheeks, but she'd forgotten for the moment what they were about.

A buzzer sounded in George's head. His thoughts fled in panic, like bandits from a burglar alarm.

"That was a real pretty dance, the dance they just did," said Hazel.

"Huh?" said George.

"That dance — it was nice."

"Yup," said George. He tried to think about the ballerinas. They weren't really very good — no better than anyone else would have been.

They were burdened with sash-weights and bags of birdshot, and their faces were masked. No one could see a free and graceful gesture or a pretty face and by comparison feel like something the cat dragged in. George was toying with a notion that maybe

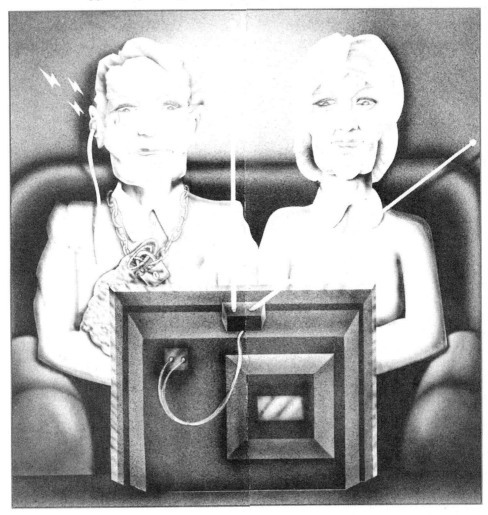

dancers shouldn't be handicapped, but a noise in his ear radio scattered his thoughts.

George winced. So did two of the eight ballerinas.

Hazel saw him wince. Having no mental handicap herself, she had to ask George what the sound had been.

"Like somebody hitting a milk bottle with a ball-peen hammer."

"I'd think it would be real interesting, hearing all the different sounds," said Hazel.

"Um," said George.

"Only, if I was Handicapper General, you know what I would do?" said Hazel. Hazel, in fact, bore a strong resemblance to the Handicapper General, a woman named Diana Moon Glampers. "If I was Diana Moon Glampers," said Hazel, "I'd have chimes on Sunday — just chimes. Kind of in honor of religion."

"I could think if it was just chimes," said George.

"Well — maybe make 'em real loud," said Hazel. "I think I'd make a good Handicapper General."

"Good as anybody else," said George.

"Who knows better'n I do what normal is?" said Hazel.

"Right," said George. He began to think glimmeringly about his abnormal son who was now in jail, about Harrison. A 21-gun salute in his head stopped that.

"Boy!" said Hazel. "That was a doozy, wasn't it?"

George was white and trembling, and tears stood on the rims of his red eyes. On the screen, the ballerinas had collapsed to the studio floor, holding their temples.

"All of a sudden you look so tired," said Hazel. "Why don't you stretch out on the sofa, so's you can rest your handicap bag on the pillows, honeybunch?" She was referring to 47 pounds of birdshot in a canvas bag, padlocked around George's neck.

George weighed the bag with his hands. "I don't mind it," he said. "I don't notice it anymore. It's just a part of me."

"You've been so tired lately — kind of wore out," said Hazel. "If there was just some way we could make a little hole in the bottom of the bag, and just take out a few of them lead balls."

"Two years in prison and a $2,000 fine for every ball I took out," said George. "That's no bargain."

"When you come home from work," said Hazel, "I mean — you don't compete with anybody around here. You just set around."

"If I tried to get away with it," said George, "then other people'd get away with it — and pretty soon we'd be right back to the dark ages again, with everybody competing against everybody else. You wouldn't like that, would you?"

"I'd hate it," said Hazel.

"There you are," said George. "When people cheat on laws, what do you think happens to society?" A siren began shrieking in his head.

"Reckon it'd fall apart," said Hazel.

"What?" said George blankly.

"Society," said Hazel uncertainly. "Isn't that what you just said?"

"Who knows?" said George.

The television program was suddenly interrupted for a news bulletin. It wasn't clear at first, since the announcer, like all announcers, had a serious speech impediment. In great excitement, he kept trying to say, "Ladies and gentlemen — " for about half a minute.

Finally he handed the bulletin to a ballerina to read.

"That's all right," Hazel said of the announcer. "He tried. He did the best he could. He should get a nice raise for trying so hard."

"Ladies and gentlemen — " said the ballerina, reading the bulletin. She must have been very beautiful, because her mask was hideous. It was easy to see that she was the strongest and most graceful of the dancers — her handicap bags were big enough for a 200-pound man. But her voice — a warm, luminous melody — was very unfair.

"Excuse me — " she said, becoming absolutely uncompetitive. "Harrison Bergeron, age 14," she said in a grackle squawk, "has just escaped from jail, where he was held on suspicion of plotting to overthrow the government. He is a genius and an athlete, is underhandicapped and extremely dangerous."

A police photograph of Harrison Bergeron was flashed on the screen — upside down, then sideways, upside down again, then right-side up. The picture showed Harrison against a background marked in feet and inches. He was seven feet tall.

The rest of Harrison's appearance was Halloween and hardware. Nobody had ever borne heavier handicaps. He had outgrown hindrances[2] faster than the H-G men could think them up. Instead of a little ear radio for a mental handicap, he wore a tremendous pair of earphones and spectacles with thick, wavy lenses. The spectacles made him half blind and gave him whanging headaches.

Scrap metal hung all over him. Ordinarily, there was neatness in handicaps issued to strong people, but Harrison looked like a walking junkyard, carrying 300 pounds.

To offset his good looks, the H-G men required that he wear a red rubber ball on his nose, keep his eyebrows shaved, and cover his teeth with black caps at random.

"If you see this boy," said the ballerina, "do not — I repeat, do not — try to reason with him."

Then came the shriek of a door being torn from hinges.

Screams and barking cries sounded from the television set. The photograph of Harrison Bergeron on the screen jumped again and again, as though dancing to an earthquake.

George Bergeron correctly identified the earthquake. Many was the time his home had danced to the same crashing tune.

"It's our boy!" said George. "That must be Harrison!"

The realization was blasted from his mind instantly by the sound of an automobile collision in his head.

When George could open his eyes again, the photograph of Harrison was gone. A living, breathing Harrison filled the screen.

Clanking and huge, Harrison stood in the center of the studio. Ballerinas, technicians, musicians, and announcers cowered on their knees.

"I am the Emperor!" cried Harrison. "Do you hear? I am the Emperor! Everybody must do what I say!" He stamped his foot.

"Even as I stand here," he bellowed, "crippled, hobbled, sickened — I am a greater ruler than any man who ever lived! Now watch me become what I can become!"

Harrison tore the straps of his handicap harness like wet tissue paper, tore straps guaranteed to support five thousand pounds. His scrap-iron handicaps crashed to the floor.

Harrison thrust his thumbs under the bar of the padlock that secured his head harness. The bar snapped like celery. He smashed headphones and spectacles against the wall.

He flung away his rubber-ball nose, revealing a man that would have awed Thor, the god of thunder.

"I shall now select my Empress!" he said, looking down on the cowering people. "Let the first woman who dares rise to her feet share my throne!"

A moment passed, and a ballerina arose, swaying like a willow.

Harrison plucked the mental handicap from her ear, snapped off her physical handicaps with marvelous delicacy. Last, he removed her mask.

She was blindingly beautiful.

Harrison took her hand. "Music!" he commanded.

The musicians scrambled back into their chairs, and Harrison stripped them of their handicaps, too. "Play your best," he said, "and I'll make you barons and dukes and earls."

The music began. It was normal at first — cheap, silly, false. Harrison snatched two musicians from their chairs, waved them like batons and sang the music as he wanted it played. He slammed them back into their chairs.

The music began again — much improved.

Harrison and his Empress listened for a while — listened

gravely, as if synchronizing their heartbeats with it. Harrison placed his big hands on the girl's tiny waist, letting her sense the weightlessness soon to be hers.

Then, in an explosion of joy and grace, into the air they sprang!

Not only were the laws of the land abandoned, but the law of gravity, the laws of motion as well.

They reeled and spun. They leaped like deer on the moon.

Each leap brought the dancers nearer to the ceiling, 30 feet above. They kissed the ceiling.

Then, neutralizing[3] gravity with love and pure will, they remained suspended in air inches below the ceiling and kissed each other.

It was then that Diana Moon Glampers, the Handicapper General, came into the studio with a double-barreled shotgun. She fired twice. The Emperor and the Empress were dead before they hit the floor.

Diana Moon Glampers loaded the gun again. She aimed it at the musicians and told them they had ten seconds to get their handicaps back on. Then the Bergerons' TV tube burned out.

Hazel turned to ask George about the blackout, but a handicap signal was shaking him up. Then he said, "You been crying?"

"Yup," she said.

"What about?" he said.

"I forgot," she said. "Something real sad on television."

"Forget sad things," said George.

"I always do," said Hazel.

"That's my girl," said George. He winced. There was the sound of a riveting gun in his head.

"Gee — I could tell that one was a doozy," said Hazel.

"You can say that again," said George.

"Gee," said Hazel, "I could tell that one was a doozy."

[1] **vigilance:** watchfulness; alertness
[2] **hindrances:** things that prevent action or make progress difficult
[3] **neutralizing:** making ineffective; counterbalancing

## A CLOSER LOOK

*1. In the year 2081, what "right" is guaranteed to all citizens by the three Constitutional Amendments? How has the government managed to make all people "equal"?*

*2. What mental handicap does George have to wear, and what purpose does it serve? Why does George have to wear the handicap, while Hazel does not?*

*3. Why is Harrison considered abnormal? Why was he put in prison?*

*4. For a few moments on television, Harrison and the ballerina show what life could be like without handicaps. Explain why their actions pose a threat to the government.*

*5. We can conclude from the story that Vonnegut is making a point about any society that tries to enforce uniformity — to make all people the same. What point is he making? Do you agree with him? Why or why not?*

• Chang Feng comes upon a beautiful meadow and lies down for a nap. But the meadow is magic. And when Chang Feng awakens, he is not quite himself.

## Li Fu-yen

# THE TIGER

*Translated by Lin Yutang*

CHANG FENG WAS TRAVELING IN FUKIEN IN THE beginning of the reign of Yuanho (806-820). He was a northerner, and the luxuriant subtropical vegetation was new and interesting to him. Among other things, he had heard of tigers in the south. One day he was stopping with his servant at an inn in Hengshan, a small town near Foochow, lying on the watershed of the high mountain ranges which divide Fukien from Chekiang. Having deposited his luggage, he went out to take in his first impressions of the land, its people and the women's costumes. Walking alone with a cane in his hand, he went on and on, attracted by the refreshing green of the country after rain, and the bracing winds which came over the mountain. He felt strangely excited. Before him lay a landscape which was a riotous display of colors. It was autumn and the hillsides literally glowed with the gold and red of maple forests. A beautiful white temple stood halfway up the mountain above a thickly wooded slope. The golden sunset transformed the mountainside and the fields into a landscape of brilliant pastels, blue and purple and green, changing in hue every moment, mingling with the dazzling red and gold. It was like a magic land.

Suddenly he felt a fainting sensation: stars danced before his eyes and his head reeled. He thought it was due to the altitude, the overexertion, and the sudden change of climate, or perhaps he was affected by the strange light. Just a few steps before him he saw a pasture land covered with velvety lawn, lying just where the wooded slope began. He took off his gown and put it with his walking stick against a tree, and lay down to take a rest. He felt a little better. As he looked up at the blue sky, he thought how beautiful and peaceful nature was. Men fought for money and

106

position and fame; they lied and cheated and killed for gain; but here was peace — in nature. As he rolled in the grass, he felt happy and relaxed. The smell of the sod and a gentle breeze soon caressed him into sleep.

When he woke up, he felt hungry and remembered it was evening. As he rolled his hands over his stomach, he touched a coating of soft fur. Quickly he sat up, and he saw his body covered with beautiful black stripes, and as he stretched his arms, he felt a delightful new strength in them, sinewy[1] and full of power. He yawned and was surprised at his own powerful roar. Looking down his own face, he saw the tips of long white whiskers. Lo, he had been transformed into a tiger!

Now, that is delightful, he thought to himself. I am no longer a man, but a tiger. It is not bad for a change.

Wanting to try his new strength, he ran into the woods and bounced from rock to rock, delighting in his new strength. He went up to the monastery,[2] and pawed at the gate, seeking admittance.

"It is a tiger!" he heard a monk inside shouting. "I smell it. Do not open!"

Now that is uncomfortable, he thought to himself. I only intended to have a simple supper and discuss Buddhist[3] philosophy with him. But of course I am a tiger now, and perhaps I do smell.

He had an instinct that he should go down the hill to the village and seek for food. As he hid behind a hedge on a country path, he saw a beautiful girl passing by, and he thought to himself, I have been told that Foochow girls are famous for their white complexion and small stature. Indeed it is true.

As he made a move to go up to the girl, she screamed and ran for her life.

What kind of a life is this, when everybody takes you for an enemy? he wondered. I will not eat her, she is so beautiful. I will take a pig, if I can find one.

At the thought of a nice, fat pig, or a small juicy lamb, his mouth watered, and he felt ashamed of himself. But there was this infernal hunger gnawing at his stomach, and he knew he had to eat something or die. He searched the village for a pig or calf, or even a chicken, but they were all under good shelters. All doors were shut against him, and as he crouched in a dark alley, waiting for a stray animal, he heard people talking inside their houses about a tiger in the village.

Unable to satisfy his hunger, he went back to the mountain, and lay in wait for some wayfarer[4] in the night. All night he waited, but nothing came his way. For a while, he must have fallen asleep.

Toward dawn, he woke up. Soon travelers began to pass along the mountain road. He saw a man coming up from the city who stopped several passengers to ask whether they had seen Cheng Chiu, a bureau chief of Foochow, who was expected to return to his office today. He was evidently a clerk from the bureau who had been sent to welcome the chief.

Something told the tiger that he must eat Cheng Chiu. Just why he must eat that person he could not tell, but the feeling was very definite that Cheng Chiu was destined to be his first victim.

"He was getting up from the inn when I left. I think he is coming behind us," he heard a man reply to the clerk's question.

"Is he traveling alone, or is he accompanied by others? Tell me his dress so that I can recognize him, for I do not want to make a mistake when I go up to greet him."

"There are three of them traveling together. The one dressed in a dark green is Cheng."

As the tiger listened to the conversation from his hiding place, it seemed as if it were taking place expressly for his benefit. He had never seen or heard of Cheng Chiu in his life. He crouched in a thicket and waited for his victim.

Soon he saw Cheng Chiu coming up the road with his secretaries, along with a group of other travelers. Cheng looked fat and juicy and delicious. When Cheng Chiu came within pouncing distance, the tiger, Chang, rushed out, felled him to the ground, and carried him up the mountain. The travelers were so frightened they all ran away. Chang's hunger was satisfied, and he only felt as if he had had a bigger breakfast than usual. He finished up the gentleman and left only the hair and bones.

Satisfied with his meal, he lay down to take a nap. When he woke up, he thought he must have been mad to eat a human being who had done him no harm. His head cleared and he decided it was not such a pleasant life, prowling night after night for food. He remembered the night before, when the instinct of hunger drove him to the village and up the mountain, and he could do nothing to stop himself.

"Why do I not go back to that lawn and see if I can become a human being again?"

He found the spot where his clothing and walking stick were still lying by the tree. He lay down again, with the wish that he might wake up to be a man once more. He rolled over on the grass, and in a few seconds found that he had been restored to his human shape.

Greatly delighted, but puzzled by the strange experience, he put on his gown, took up his cane, and started back to the town. When he reached the inn, he found he had been away exactly twenty-four hours.

"Where have you been, Master?" asked his servant, "I have been out looking for you all day." The innkeeper also came up to speak to him, evidently relieved to see him return.

"We have been worried about you," said the innkeeper. "There was a tiger abroad. He was seen by a girl in the village last night, and this morning Cheng Chiu, a bureau chief who was returning to his office, was eaten by him."

Chang Feng made up a story that he had spent the night discussing Buddhist philosophy up in the temple.

"You are lucky!" cried the innkeeper, shaking his head. "It was in that neighborhood that Cheng Chiu was killed by the tiger."

"No, the tiger will not eat me," Chang Feng replied.

"Why not?"

"He cannot," said Chang Feng enigmatically.[5]

Chang Feng kept the secret to himself, for he could not afford to tell anybody that he had eaten a man. It would be embarrassing, to say the least.

He went back to his home in Honan, and a few years went by. One day he was stopping at Huaiyang, a city on the Huai River. His friends gave him a dinner and much wine was consumed, as was usual on such occasions. Between the courses and the sipping of wine, the guests were each asked to tell a strange experience, and if in the opinion of the company the story was not strange enough, the teller of the story was to be fined a cup of wine.

Chang Feng began to tell his own story, and it happened that one of the guests was the son of Cheng Chiu, the man he had eaten. As he proceeded with his story, the young man's face grew angrier and angrier.

"So it was you who killed my father!" the young man shouted at him, his eyes distended[6] and the veins standing up on his temples.

Chang Feng hastily stood up and apologized. He knew he had got into a very serious situation. "I am sorry. I did not know it was your father."

The young man suddenly whipped out a knife and threw it at him. Luckily it missed and fell with a clang on the floor. The young man made a rush at him, and would have fallen on him, but the guests, greatly disturbed by the sudden turn of events, held him back.

"I will kill you to avenge my father's death. I will follow you to the ends of the earth!" the young man shouted.

The friends persuaded Chang Feng to leave the house at once and hide himself for a while, while they tried to calm Cheng Chiu's son. It was conceded[7] by everybody that to avenge one's father's death was a noble and laudable[8] undertaking, but after all, Chang Feng had eaten Cheng Chiu when he was a tiger, and no one wanted to see more blood shed. It was a novel situation and posed a complicated moral problem as to whether revenge under such circumstances was justified. The youth still swore murder to appease[9] his father's spirit.

In the end, the friends spoke to the commander of the region who ordered the young man to cross the Huai River and never return to the northern bank, while Chang Feng changed his name and went to the northwest to keep as far away from his sworn enemy as possible.

When the young man returned to his home, his friends said to him, "We entirely sympathize with your determination to avenge your father. That is a son's duty, of course. However, Chang Feng ate your father when he was a tiger and not responsible for his action. He did not know your father and had no purpose in killing him. That was a strange and special case, but it was not intentional murder, and if you kill him, you will be tried for murder yourself."

The son respected this advice and did not pursue Chang Feng anymore.

[1] **sinewy:** vigorous; strong
[2] **monastery:** a building where religious persons, especially monks, live
[3] **Buddhist:** eastern and central Asian religion based on the teachings of Buddha
[4] **wayfarer:** traveler
[5] **enigmatically:** mysteriously
[6] **distended:** bulging; enlarged
[7] **conceded:** admitted; acknowledged
[8] **laudable:** praiseworthy
[9] **appease:** satisfy; make calm

## A CLOSER LOOK

*1. What does Chang Feng find delightful about being a tiger? How does he finally satisfy his hunger? How does he feel about what he has done? Why does he decide that being a tiger is not such a pleasant life after all?*

*2. The son of the man Chang Feng ate wants to avenge his father's death by killing Chang Feng. This "posed a complicated moral problem as to whether revenge under such circumstances was justified." Explain the moral problem.*

*3. The young man's friends decide that Chang Feng should not be held responsible for what he did when he was a tiger. Do you agree with their decision? Why or why not?*

*4. Do you think Chang Feng really turned into a tiger? Or was the whole episode just a dream? Support your answer with evidence from the story.*

● "The Last Leaf" takes place in a section of New York City called Greenwich Village. In 1907, when the story was written, the Village was just beginning to turn into an artists' colony. You can tell by the way he describes it that O. Henry is fond of Greenwich Village. He views its people as well as its quaint streets and buildings with an affectionate humor. His description of the Village sets the atmosphere of the story, and this atmosphere leads you to expect something heartwarming. You will not be disappointed.

## O. Henry

# THE LAST LEAF

IN A LITTLE DISTRICT WEST OF WASHINGTON Square the streets have run crazy and broken themselves into small strips called "places." These "places" make strange angles and curves. One street crosses itself a time or two. An artist once discovered a valuable possibility in this street. Suppose a collector with a bill for paints, paper, and canvas should, in traversing this route, suddenly meet himself coming back, without a cent having been paid on account.

So, to quaint old Greenwich Village the art people soon came prowling, hunting for north windows and eighteenth-century gables and Dutch attics and low rents. Then they imported some pewter mugs and a chafing dish or two from Sixth Avenue, and became a "colony."

At the top of a squatty, three-story brick Sue and Johnsy had their studio. "Johnsy" was familiar for Joanna. One was from Maine, the other from California. They had met at the *table d'hôte*[1] of an Eighth Street "Delmonico's,"[2] and found their tastes in art, chicory salad, and bishop sleeves so congenial[3] that the joint studio resulted.

That was in May. In November a cold, unseen stranger, whom the doctors called Pneumonia, stalked about the colony, touching one here and there with his icy fingers. Over on the East Side this ravager strode boldly, smiting[4] his victims by scores, but his feet trod slowly through the maze of the narrow and moss-grown "places."

Mr. Pneumonia was not what you would call a chivalric old gentleman. A mite of a little woman with blood thinned by California zephyrs[5] was hardly fair game for the red-fisted, short-breathed old duffer. But Johnsy he smote; and she lay, scarcely moving, on her painted iron bedstead, looking through the small Dutch window-panes at the blank side of the next brick house.

One morning the busy doctor invited Sue into the hallway with a shaggy, gray eyebrow.

"She has one chance in — let us say, ten," he said, as he shook down the mercury in his clinical thermometer. "And that chance is for her to want to live. This way people have of lining up on the side of the undertaker makes the entire pharmacopoeia[6] look silly. Your little lady has made up her mind that she's not going to get well. Has she anything on her mind?"

"She — she wanted to paint the Bay of Naples some day," said Sue.

"Paint? — bosh! Has she anything on her mind worth thinking about twice — a man, for instance?"

"A man?" said Sue, with a jew's-harp twang in her voice. "Is a man worth — but, no, doctor; there is nothing of the kind."

"Well, it is the weakness, then," said the doctor. "I will do all that science, so far as it may filter through my efforts, can accomplish. But whenever my patient begins to count the carriages in her funeral procession I subtract 50 percent from the curative power of medicines. If you will get her to ask one question about the new winter styles in cloak sleeves I will promise you a one-in-five chance for her, instead of one in ten."

After the doctor had gone Sue went into the workroom and cried a Japanese napkin to a pulp. Then she swaggered into Johnsy's room with her drawing board, whistling ragtime.

Johnsy lay, scarcely making a ripple under the bedclothes, with her face toward the window. Sue stopped whistling, thinking she was asleep.

She arranged her board and began a pen-and-ink drawing to illustrate a magazine story. Young artists must pave their way to Art by drawing pictures for magazine stories that young authors write to pave their way to Literature.

As Sue was sketching a pair of elegant horseshow riding trousers and a monocle on the figure of the hero, an Idaho cowboy, she heard a low sound, several times repeated. She went quickly to the bedside.

Johnsy's eyes were open wide. She was looking out the window and counting — counting backward.

"Twelve," she said, and a little later "eleven"; and then "ten," and "nine"; and then "eight" and "seven," almost together.

Sue looked solicitously[7] out of the window. What was there to count? There was only a bare, dreary yard to be seen, and the blank side of the brick house twenty feet away. An old, old ivy vine, gnarled and decayed at the roots, climbed half way up the brick wall. The cold breath of autumn had stricken its leaves from the vine until its skeleton branches clung, almost bare, to the crumbling bricks.

"What is it, dear?" asked Sue.

"Six," said Johnsy, in almost a whisper. "They're falling faster now. Three days ago there were almost a hundred. It made my head ache to count them. But now it's easy. There goes another one. There are only five left now."

"Five what, dear? Tell your Sudie."

"Leaves. On the ivy vine. When the last one falls I must go, too. I've known that for three days. Didn't the doctor tell you?"

"Oh, I never heard of such nonsense," complained Sue, with magnificent scorn. "What have old ivy leaves to do with your getting well? And you used to love that vine so, you naughty girl. Don't be a goosey. Why, the doctor told me this morning that your chances for getting well real soon were — let's see exactly what he said — he said the chances were ten to one! Why, that's almost as good a chance as we have in New York when we ride on the street cars or walk past a new building. Try to take some broth now, and let Sudie go back to her drawing, so she can sell the editor man with it, and buy port wine for her sick child, and pork chops for her greedy self."

"You needn't get any more wine," said Johnsy, keeping her eyes fixed out the window. "There goes another. No, I don't want any broth. That leaves just four. I want to see the last one fall before it gets dark. Then I'll go, too."

"Johnsy, dear," said Sue, bending over her, "will you promise me to keep your eyes closed, and not look out the window until I am done working? I must hand those drawings in by tomorrow. I need the light, or I would draw the shade down."

"Couldn't you draw in the other room?" asked Johnsy, coldly.

"I'd rather be here by you," said Sue. "Besides, I don't want you to keep looking at those silly ivy leaves."

"Tell me as soon as you have finished," said Johnsy, closing her eyes, and lying white and still as a fallen statue, "because I want to see the last one fall. I'm tired of waiting. I'm tired of thinking. I want to turn loose my hold on everything, and go sailing down, down, just like one of those poor, tired leaves."

"Try to sleep," said Sue. "I must call Behrman up to be my model for the old hermit miner. I'll not be gone a minute. Don't try to move 'til I come back."

Old Behrman was a painter who lived on the ground floor beneath them. He was past sixty and had a Michael Angelo's Moses beard curling down from the head of a satyr[8] along the body of an imp. Behrman was a failure in art. Forty years he had wielded the brush without getting near enough to touch the hem of his Mistress's robe. He had been always about to paint a masterpiece, but had never yet begun it. For several years he had painted nothing except now and then a daub in the line of commerce or advertising. He earned a little by serving as a model to those young artists in the colony who could not pay the price of a professional. He drank gin to excess, and still talked of his coming masterpiece. For the rest he was a fierce little old man, who scoffed terribly at softness in anyone, and who regarded himself as especial mastiff-in-waiting[9] to protect the two young artists in the studio above.

Sue found Behrman smelling strongly of juniper berries in his dimly lighted den below. In one corner was a blank canvas on an easel that had been waiting there for twenty-five years to receive the first line of the masterpiece. She told him of Johnsy's fancy, and how she feared she would, indeed, light and fragile as a leaf herself, float away, when her slight hold upon the world grew weaker.

Old Behrman, with his red eyes plainly streaming, shouted his contempt and derision for such idiotic imaginings.

"Vass!" he cried. "Is dere people in de world mit der foolishness to die because leafs dey drop off from a confounded vine? I haf not heard of such a thing. No, I will not bose as a model for your fool hermit-dunder-head. Vy do you allow dot silly pusiness to come in der brain of her?"

"She is very ill and weak," said Sue, "and the fever has left her mind morbid[10] and full of strange fancies.[11] Very well, Mr. Behrman, if you do not care to pose for me, you needn't. But I think you are a horrid old — old flibbertigibbet."

"You are just like a woman!" yelled Behrman. "Who said I will

115

not bose? Go on. I come mit you. For half an hour I haf peen trying to say dot I am ready to bose. Gott! dis is not any blace in which one so goot as Miss Yohnsy shall lie sick. Some day I vill baint a masterpiece, and ve shall all go away. Gott! yes."

Johnsy was sleeping when they went upstairs. Sue pulled the shade down to the windowsill, and motioned Behrman into the other room. In there they peered out the window fearfully at the ivy vine. Then they looked at each other for a moment without speaking. A persistent, cold rain was falling, mingled with snow. Behrman, in his old blue shirt, took his seat as the hermit miner on an upturned kettle for a rock.

When Sue awoke from an hour's sleep the next morning she found Johnsy with dull, wide-open eyes staring at the drawn green shade.

"Pull it up; I want to see," she ordered, in a whisper.

Wearily Sue obeyed.

But, lo! after the beating rain and fierce gusts of wind that had endured through the livelong night, there yet stood out against the brick wall one ivy leaf. It was the last on the vine. Still dark green near its stem, but with its serrated[12] edges tinted with the yellow of dissolution[13] and decay, it hung bravely from a branch some twenty feet above the ground.

"It is the last one," said Johnsy. "I thought it would surely fall during the night. I heard the wind. It will fall today, and I shall die at the same time."

"Dear, dear," said Sue, leaning her worn face down to the pillow, "think of me, if you won't think of yourself. What would I do?"

But Johnsy did not answer. The lonesomest thing in all the world is a soul when it is making ready to go on its mysterious, far journey. The fancy seemed to possess her more strongly as one by one the ties that bound her to friendship and to earth were loosed.

The day wore away, and even through the twilight they could see the lone ivy leaf clinging to its stem against the wall. And then, with the coming of the night the north wind was again loosed, while the rain still beat against the windows and pattered down from the low Dutch eaves.

When it was light enough Johnsy, the merciless, commanded that the shade be raised.

The ivy leaf was still there.

Johnsy lay for a long time looking at it. And then she called to

Sue, who was stirring her chicken broth over the gas stove.

"I've been a bad girl, Sudie," said Johnsy. "Something has made that last leaf stay there to show me how wicked I was. It is a sin to want to die. You may bring me a little broth now, and some milk with a little port in it, and — no; bring me a hand-mirror first, and then pack some pillows about me, and I will sit up and watch you cook."

An hour later she said:

"Sudie, some day I hope to paint the Bay of Naples."

The doctor came in the afternoon, and Sue had an excuse to go into the hall as he left.

"Even chances," said the doctor, taking Sue's thin, shaking hand in his. "With good nursing you'll win. And now I must see another case I have downstairs. Behrman, his name is —

some kind of an artist, I believe. Pneumonia, too. He is an old, weak man, and the attack is acute.[14] There is no hope for him; but he goes to the hospital today to be made more comfortable."

The next day the doctor said to Sue: "She's out of danger. You've won. Nutrition and care now — that's all."

And that afternoon Sue came to the bed where Johnsy lay, contentedly knitting a very blue and very useless wool scarf, and put one arm around her, pillows and all.

"I have something to tell you, white mouse," she said. "Mr. Behrman died of pneumonia today in the hospital. He was ill only two days. The janitor found him on the morning of the first day in his room downstairs helpless with pain. His shoes and clothing were wet through and icy cold. They couldn't imagine where he had been on such a dreadful night. And then they found a lantern, still lighted, and a ladder that had been dragged from its place, and some scattered brushes, and a palette with green and yellow colors mixed on it, and — look out the window, dear, at the last ivy leaf on the wall. Didn't you wonder why it never fluttered or moved when the wind blew? Ah, darling, it's Behrman's masterpiece — he painted it there the night that the last leaf fell."

1 *table d'hôte:* a complete meal served at a stated time and fixed price
2 **Delmonico's:** a fashionable and expensive restaurant in New York. The "Delmonico's" where Sue and Johnsy met was probably a boarding house.
3 **congenial:** pleasingly similar
4 **smiting:** striking hard, as if by heavy blows
5 **zephyrs:** breezes from the west
6 **pharmacopoeia:** stock of drugs and medicines available to doctors
7 **solicitously:** with concern or apprehension
8 **satyr:** mythical creature, part man and part goat, that enjoyed drinking and having a good time
9 **mastiff-in-waiting:** guard dog
10 **morbid:** gloomy
11 **fancies:** ideas or notions
12 **serrated:** notched
13 **dissolution:** disintegration
14 **acute:** severe

## A CLOSER LOOK

*1. The doctor tells Sue that Johnsy has one chance to live. What is that one chance? On what object does Johnsy's life depend?*

*2. To advance the plot, it is necessary to inform Old Behrman about Johnsy's condition and about her idea that she will die when the last leaf falls. O. Henry could have had Sue run into Behrman by accident and tell him about Johnsy. But his device for getting the information to Behrman is neater than that, and it does not depend on coincidence. What device does he use?*

*3. Why does Johnsy finally decide to make an effort to live? Why doesn't the last leaf fall?*

*4. What is Old Behrman's life's goal? What price does he pay to achieve it? Suppose he had already painted many masterpieces. Would the price he paid for painting just one more have seemed too high? Now consider the fact that the painting of the last leaf is Behrman's one and only masterpiece. Explain why that fact makes it easier for us to accept his death.*

# PART III

# CHARACTER

A story is believable when the personality traits of its characters provide convincing motives for their behavior. Therefore, good writers take great pains to make their characters seem vivid and lifelike. There are two methods an author can use to achieve this effect.

1. The author can portray a character directly, as O. Henry did Behrman in "The Last Leaf." O. Henry stated that Behrman was a failure; old; fierce in manner.

2. Or, the author can portray a character indirectly, through what the character says, does, and thinks, and through what other characters say and think about him. O. Henry uses the indirect method, too, in portraying Behrman. For, after stating that Behrman despises weakness, he shows him "with his red eyes plainly streaming" tears on hearing of Johnsy's illness. We conclude from this evidence that Behrman's ferocity is all bluff, and that underneath he is softhearted.

The scene on the left is another close-up from the picture on pages 4-5. Suppose the artist in this scene were a character in a story. The author might portray the character directly by stating that he is a talented artist with a sense of humor. Or, the author might portray him indirectly through the onlooker's thoughts or comments about the artist and his work.

In this scene, the artist is the most important element because he is the one who is taking action. And, in the stories that follow, the characters are the most important element because everything that happens hinges on what they are and what they do.

• "Saki" is the pen name of Hector Hugh Munro, a Scottish writer who lived from 1870 to 1916. He is best known for his cleverly worked out plots and his witty exposure of some of the less admirable aspects of human nature. Stinginess, pretentiousness, and hypocrisy are his targets in "Mrs. Packletide's Tiger," which takes place in India while it was still a British colony. As you read the story, notice the small, bright touches of wit. Much of the wit is ironic; it is Saki's way of reminding the reader that what people pretend to be is often the opposite of what they are.

# Saki

# MRS. PACKLETIDE'S TIGER

IT WAS MRS. PACKLETIDE'S PLEASURE AND INTEN-
tion that she should shoot a tiger. Not that the lust to kill had suddenly descended on her, or that she felt that she would leave India safer and more wholesome than she had found it, with one fraction less of wild beast per million of inhabitants. The compelling motive for her sudden deviation[1] toward the footsteps of Nimrod[2] was the fact that Loona Bimberton had recently been carried eleven miles in an airplane by an Algerian aviator, and talked of nothing else; only a personally procured[3] tiger skin and a heavy harvest of press photographs could successfully counter that sort of thing. Mrs. Packletide had already arranged in her mind the lunch she would give at her house in Curzon Street, ostensibly[4] in Loona Bimberton's honor, with a tiger-skin rug occupying most of the foreground and all of the conversation. She had also already designed in her mind the tiger-claw brooch[5] that she was going to give Loona Bimberton on her next birthday. In a world that is supposed to be chiefly swayed by hunger and by love Mrs. Packletide was an exception; her movements and motives were, to a great extent, governed by dislike of Loona Bimberton.

Circumstances proved propitious.[6] Mrs. Packletide had offered a thousand rupees[7] for the opportunity of shooting a tiger without overmuch risk or exertion, and it so happened that a neighboring village could boast of being the favored rendezvous[8] of an animal of respectable antecedents,[9] which had been driven by the increasing infirmities[10] of age to abandon game-killing and confine its appetite to the smaller domestic animals. The prospect of earning the thousand rupees had stimulated the sporting and commercial instinct of the villagers; children were posted night and day on the outskirts of the local jungle to head the tiger back in the unlikely event of his attempting to roam away to fresh hunting-grounds, and the cheaper kinds of goats were left about with elaborate careless-ness to keep him satisfied with his present quarters.

The one great anxiety was lest he should die of old age before the date appointed for the memsahib's[11] shoot. Mothers carrying their babies home through the jungle after the day's work in the fields hushed their singing lest they might curtail the restful sleep of the venerable herd-robber.

The great night duly arrived, moonlit and cloudless. A platform had been constructed in a comfortable and conveniently placed tree, and thereon crouched Mrs. Packletide and her paid compan-ion, Miss Mebbin. A goat, gifted with a particularly persistent bleat, such as even a partially deaf tiger might be reasonably expected to hear on a still night, was tethered at the correct distance. With an accurately sighted rifle and a thumb-nail pack of patience cards,[12] the sportswoman awaited the coming of the quarry.[13]

"I suppose we are in some danger?" said Miss Mebbin.

She was not actually nervous about the wild beast, but she had a morbid dread of performing an atom more service than she had been paid for.

"Nonsense," said Mrs. Packletide; "it's a very old tiger. It couldn't spring up here even if it wanted to."

"If it's an old tiger I think you ought to get it cheaper. A thousand rupees is a lot of money."

Louisa Mebbin adopted a protective elder-sister attitude toward money in general, irrespective of nationality or denomination.[14] Her energetic intervention had saved many a ruble from dissipat-ing[15] itself in tips in some Moscow hotel, and francs and centimes clung to her instinctively under circumstances which would have driven them headlong from less sympathetic hands. Her specula-tions as to the market depreciation[16] of tiger remnants were cut short by the appearance on the scene of the animal itself. As soon as it caught sight of the tethered[17] goat it lay flat on the earth, seemingly less from a desire to take advantage of all available cover than for the purpose of snatching a short rest before com-

mencing the grand attack.

"I believe it's ill," said Louisa Mebbin, loudly in Hindustani, for the benefit of the village headman, who was in ambush in a neighboring tree.

"Hush!" said Mrs. Packletide, and at that moment the tiger commenced ambling toward his victim.

"Now, now!" urged Miss Mebbin with some excitement; "if he doesn't touch the goat we needn't pay for it." (The bait was an extra.)

The rifle flashed out with a loud report, and the great tawny beast sprang to one side and then rolled over in the stillness of death. In a moment a crowd of excited natives had swarmed on to the scene, and their shouting speedily carried the glad news to the village, where a thumping of tom-toms took up the chorus of triumph. And their triumph and rejoicing found a ready echo in the heart of Mrs. Packletide; already that luncheon-party in Curzon Street seemed immeasurably nearer.

It was Louisa Mebbin who drew attention to the fact that the goat was in death-throes from a mortal bullet-wound, while no trace of the rifle's deadly work could be found on the tiger. Evidently the wrong animal had been hit, and the beast of prey had succumbed to heart-failure, caused by the sudden report of the rifle, accelerated by senile decay. Mrs. Packletide was pardonably annoyed at the discovery; but, at any rate, she was the possessor of a dead tiger, and the villagers, anxious for their thousand rupees, gladly connived[18] at the fiction that she had shot the beast. And Miss Mebbin was a paid companion. Therefore did Mrs. Packletide face the cameras with a light heart, and her pictured fame reached from the pages of the *Texas Weekly Snapshot* to the illustrated Monday supplement of the *Novoe Vremya*. As for Loona Bimberton, she refused to look at an illustrated paper for weeks, and her letter of thanks for the gift of a tiger-claw brooch was a model of repressed emotions. The luncheon-party she declined; there are limits beyond which repressed emotions become dangerous.

From Curzon Street the tiger-skin rug traveled down to the Manor House, and was duly inspected and admired by the county, and it seemed a fitting and appropriate thing when Mrs. Packletide went to the County Costume Ball in the character of Diana.[19] She refused to fall in, however, with Clovis's[20] tempting suggestion of a primeval[21] dance party, at which everyone should wear the skins of beasts they had recently slain. "I should be in rather a Baby Bunting condition," confessed Clovis, "with a miserable rabbit-skin or two to wrap up in, but then," he added, with a rather malicious glance at Diana's proportions, "my figure is quite as good as that Russian dancing boy's."

"How amused everyone would be if they knew what really

happened," said Louisa Mebbin a few days after the ball.

"What do you mean?" asked Mrs. Packletide quickly.

"How you shot the goat and frightened the tiger to death," said Miss Mebbin, with her disagreeably pleasant laugh.

"No one would believe it," said Mrs. Packletide, her face changing color as rapidly as though it were going through a book of patterns[22] before post time.[23]

"Loona Bimberton would," said Miss Mebbin. Mrs. Packletide's face settled on an unbecoming shade of greenish white.

"You surely wouldn't give me away?" she asked.

"I've seen a weekend cottage near Dorking that I should rather like to buy," said Miss Mebbin with seeming irrelevance.[24] "Six hundred and eighty, freehold.[25] Quite a bargain, only I don't have the money."

Louisa Mebbin's pretty weekend cottage, christened by her "Les Fauves,"[26] and gay in summertime with its garden borders of tiger-lilies, is the wonder and admiration of her friends.

"It is a marvel how Louisa manages to do it," is the general verdict.

Mrs. Packletide indulges in no more big-game shooting.

"The incidental expenses[27] are so heavy," she confides to inquiring friends.

1 **deviation:** departure from normal behavior
2 **Nimrod:** a Biblical figure famed as a mighty hunter
3 **procured:** obtained; acquired
4 **ostensibly:** apparently; on the face of it
5 **brooch:** an ornamental pin
6 **propitious:** favorable
7 **rupees:** Indian currency
8 **rendezvous:** retreat or refuge
9 **antecedents:** ancestors
10 **infirmities:** weaknesses
11 **memsahib:** a European woman living in India
12 **thumbnail pack of patience cards:** miniature cards for playing solitaire
13 **quarry:** animal chased in a hunt
14 **denomination:** value
15 **dissipating:** wasting
16 **depreciation:** lowering in price or value
17 **tethered:** tied up
18 **connived:** cooperated secretly
19 **Diana:** in Roman mythology, the goddess of the hunt
20 **Clovis:** a character in *The Chronicles of Clovis*, a group of stories that includes "Mrs. Packletide's Tiger."
21 **primeval:** relating to the earliest times
22 **book of patterns:** book showing the color-patterns of racing stables; these colors are worn by jockeys
23 **post time:** the start of a horse race and the deadline for placing a bet
24 **irrelevance:** unconnected to the matter at hand
25 **freehold:** owned, as distinguished from leased or rented
26 **"Les Fauves":** French for "The Wild Animals"
27 **incidental expenses:** extra costs connected with the pursuit of some activity, beyond the costs of the activity itself

## A CLOSER LOOK

*1. What is Mrs. Packletide's main reason for wanting to shoot a tiger? Why does she give Loona Bimberton a tiger-claw brooch?*

*2. Incidental expenses are extra costs connected with the pursuit of some activity, beyond the basic expenses of the activity itself. The thousand rupees that Mrs. Packletide pays for the opportunity to shoot a tiger is a basic expense. What is the incidental expense that she pays as well?*

*3. Mrs. Packletide sets out to put one over on Loona Bimberton. In the end, Louisa Mebbin puts one over on Mrs. Packletide. Not only does she succeed in blackmailing her employer, but she also flaunts her success. Think about the name Miss Mebbin gives her cottage ("Les Fauves," or "The Wild Animals") and the tiger-lilies she plants in her garden. Then explain why both the name and the flowers would annoy Mrs. Packletide.*

● Mr. Beelzy[1] said he wouldn't let anybody hurt the little boy. But Mr. Beelzy is just an imaginary playmate . . . isn't he?

## John Collier

# THUS I REFUTE BEELZY

"THERE GOES THE TEA BELL," SAID MRS. Carter. "I hope Simon hears it."

They looked out from the window of the drawing-room. The long garden, agreeably neglected, ended in a waste plot. Here a little summer-house was passing close by beauty on its way to complete decay. This was Simon's retreat. It was almost completely screened by the tangled branches of the apple tree and the pear tree, planted too close together, as they always are in the suburbs. They caught a glimpse of him now and then, as he strutted up and down, mouthing and gesticulating,[2] performing all the solemn mumbo-jumbo of small boys who spend long afternoons at the forgotten ends of long gardens.

"There he is, bless him!" said Betty.

"Playing his game," said Mrs. Carter. "He won't play with the other children any more. And if I go down there — the temper! And comes in tired out!"

"He doesn't have his sleep in the afternoons?" asked Betty.

"You know what Big Simon's ideas are," said Mrs. Carter. " 'Let him choose for himself,' he says. That's what he chooses, and he comes in as white as a sheet."

"Look! He's heard the bell," said Betty. The expression was justified, though the bell had ceased ringing a full minute ago. Small Simon stopped in his parade exactly as if its tinny dingle had at that moment reached his ear. They watched him perform certain ritual[3] sweeps and scratchings with his little stick, and come lagging over the hot and flaggy grass toward the house.

Mrs. Carter led the way down to the playroom, or garden-room, which was also the tea-room for hot days. It had been the huge scullery[4] of this tall Georgian house. Now the walls were cream-washed, there was coarse blue net in the windows, canvas-covered armchairs on the stone floor, and a reproduction of Van Gogh's

130

*Sunflowers* over the mantelpiece.

Small Simon came drifting in, and accorded Betty a perfunctory[5] greeting. His face was an almost perfect triangle, pointed at the chin, and he was paler than he should have been.

"The little elf-child!"[6] cried Betty.

Simon looked at her. "No," said he.

At that moment the door opened, and Mr. Carter came in,

rubbing his hands. He was a dentist, and washed them before and after everything he did. "You!" said his wife. "Home already!"

"Not unwelcome, I hope," said Mr. Carter, nodding to Betty. "Two people canceled their appointments: I decided to come home. I said, I hope I am not unwelcome."

"Silly!" said his wife. "Of course not."

"Small Simon seems doubtful," continued Mr. Carter. "Small Simon, are you sorry to see me at tea with you?"

"No, Daddy."

"No, what?"

"No, Big Simon."

"That's right. Big Simon and Small Simon. That sounds more like friends, doesn't it? At one time little boys had to call their father 'sir.' If they forgot — a good spanking. On the bottom, Small Simon! On the bottom!" said Mr. Carter, washing his hands once more with his invisible soap and water.

The little boy turned crimson with shame or rage.

"But now, you see," said Betty, to help, "you can call your father whatever you like."

"And what," asked Mr. Carter, "has Small Simon been doing this afternoon? While Big Simon has been at work."

"Nothing," muttered his son.

"Then you have been bored," said Mr. Carter. "Learn from experience, Small Simon. Tomorrow, do something amusing, and you will not be bored. I want him to learn from experience, Betty. That is my way, the new way."

"I have learned," said the boy, speaking like an old, tired man, as little boys so often do.

"It would hardly seem so," said Mr. Carter, "if you sit on your behind all the afternoon, doing nothing. Had my father caught me doing nothing, I should not have sat very comfortably."

"He played," said Mrs. Carter.

"A bit," said the boy, shifting on his chair.

"Too much," said Mrs. Carter. "He comes in all nervy and dazed. He ought to have his rest."

"He is six," said her husband. "He is a reasonable being. He must choose for himself. But what game is this, Small Simon, that is worth getting nervy and dazed over? There are very few games as good as all that."

"It's nothing," said the boy.

"Oh, come," said his father. "We are friends, are we not? You can tell me. I was a Small Simon once, just like you, and played the same games you play. Of course there were no airplanes in those days. With whom do you play this fine game? Come on, we must all answer civil questions, or the world would never go round. With whom do you play?"

"Mr. Beelzy," said the boy, unable to resist.

"Mr. Beelzy?" said his father, raising his eyebrows inquiringly at his wife.

"It's a game he makes up," said she.

"Not makes up!" cried the boy. "Fool!"

"That is telling stories," said his mother. "And rude as well. We had better talk of something different."

"No wonder he is rude," said Mr. Carter, "if you say he tells lies, and then insist on changing the subject. He tells you his fantasy: you implant a guilt feeling. What can you expect? A defense mechanism.[7] Then you get a real lie."

"Like in *These Three,*"[8] said Betty. "Only different, of course. *She* was an unblushing little liar."

"I would have made her blush," said Mr. Carter, "in the proper part of her anatomy. But Small Simon is in the fantasy stage. Are you not, Small Simon? You just make things up."

"No, I don't," said the boy.

"You do," said his father. "And because you do, it is not too late to reason with you. There is no harm in a fantasy, old chap. There is no harm in a bit of make-believe. Only you have to know the difference between daydreams and real things, or your brain will never grow. It will never be the brain of a Big Simon. So come on. Let us hear about this Mr. Beelzy of yours. Come on. What is he like?"

"He isn't like anything," said the boy.

"Like nothing on earth?" said his father. "That's a terrible fellow."

"I'm not frightened of him," said the child, smiling. "Not a bit."

"I should hope not," said his father. "If you were, you would be frightening yourself. I am always telling people, older people than you are, that they are just frightening themselves. Is he a funny man? Is he a giant?"

"Sometimes he is," said the little boy.

"Sometimes one thing, sometimes another," said his father. "Sounds pretty vague. Why can't you tell us what he's like?"

"I love him," said the boy. "He loves me."

"That's a big word," said Mr. Carter. "That might be better kept for real things, like Big Simon and Small Simon."

"He is real," said the boy, passionately. "He's not a fool. He's real."

"Listen," said his father. "When you go down the garden there's nobody there. Is there?"

"No," said the boy.

"Then you think of him, inside your head, and he comes."

"No," said Small Simon. "I have to make marks. On the ground. With my stick."

"That doesn't matter."

"Yes, it does."

"Small Simon, you are being obstinate," said Mr. Carter. "I am trying to explain something to you. I have been longer in the world than you have, so naturally I am older and wiser. I am explaining that Mr. Beelzy is a fantasy of yours. Do you hear? Do you understand?"

"Yes, Daddy."

"He is a game. He is a let's-pretend."

The little boy looked down at his plate, smiling resignedly.

"I hope you are listening to me," said his father. "All you have to do is to say, 'I have been playing a game of let's-pretend. With someone I make up, called Mr. Beelzy.' Then no one will say you tell lies, and you will know the difference between dreams and reality. Mr. Beelzy is a daydream."

The little boy still stared at his plate.

"He is sometimes there and sometimes not there," pursued Mr. Carter. "Sometimes he's like one thing, sometimes another. You can't really see him. You can touch me. I can touch you." Mr. Carter stretched out his big, white, dentist's hand, and took his little son by the nape of the neck. He stopped speaking for a moment and tightened his hand. The little boy sank his head still lower.

"Now you know the difference," said Mr. Carter, "between a pretend and a real thing. You and I are one thing; he is another. Which is the pretend? Come on. Answer me. What is the pretend?"

"Big Simon and Small Simon," said the little boy.

"Don't!" cried Betty, and at once put her hand over her mouth, for why should a visitor cry "Don't!" when a father is explaining

things in a scientific and modern way? Besides, it annoys the father.

"Well, my boy," said Mr. Carter, "I have said you must be allowed to learn from experience. Go upstairs. Right up to your room. You shall learn whether it is better to reason, or to be perverse[9] and obstinate. Go up. I shall follow you."

"You are not going to beat the child?" cried Mrs. Carter.

"No," said the little boy. "Mr. Beelzy won't let him."

"Go on up with you!" shouted his father.

Small Simon stopped at the door. "He said he wouldn't let anyone hurt me," he whimpered. "He said he'd come like a lion, with wings on, and eat them up."

"You'll learn how real he is!" shouted his father after him. "If you can't learn it at one end, you shall learn it at the other. I'll have your breeches down. I shall finish my cup of tea first, however," said he to the two women.

Neither of them spoke. Mr. Carter finished his tea, and unhurriedly left the room, washing his hands with his invisible soap and water.

Mrs. Carter said nothing. Betty could think of nothing to say. She wanted to be talking for she was afraid of what they might hear.

135

Suddenly it came. It seemed to tear the air apart. "Good God!" she cried. "What was that? He's hurt him." She sprang out of her chair, her silly eyes flashing behind her glasses. "I'm going up there!" she cried, trembling.

"Yes, let us go up." said Mrs. Carter. "Let us go up. That was not Small Simon."

It was on the second-floor landing that they found the shoe, with the man's foot still in it, like that last morsel[10] of a mouse which sometimes falls unnoticed from the side of the jaws of the cat.

[1] **Beelzy:** Beelzebub, one of the angels who, with Satan, were expelled from heaven for disobedience to God

[2] **gesticulating:** gesturing in a lively or excited way

[3] **ritual:** ceremonial act or action

[4] **scullery:** room for cleaning and storing dishes, washing vegetables, and similar work

[5] **perfunctory:** done mechanically; lacking in interest or enthusiasm

[6] **elf-child:** a changeling, or fairy-infant, left by elves in exchange for a human child they have stolen

[7] **defense mechanism:** a psychological term referring to an unconscious process that protects an individual from unacceptable ideas or impulses

[8] *These Three:* a 1936 movie involving a girl whose malicious lies cause trouble

[9] **perverse:** contrary; willful

[10] **morsel:** mouthful or small bite

## A CLOSER LOOK

*1. The long-term, ongoing conflict in this story is between Small Simon's desire to be himself and his father's determination to turn him into an adult like himself. What is the short-term, specific conflict? Or, to put the question another way, what quarrel is decided at the end of the story?*

*2. What kind of relationship does Big Simon claim to want with his son? Do you believe he really wants such a relationship? Support your answer with evidence from the story.*

*3. Mr. Beelzy will eat up anybody who tries to hurt me, Small Simon tells his father. Does Mr. Beelzy keep his promise? What happens to the father at the end of the story?*

*4. Although the story is clearly a fantasy, the author makes the characters seem lifelike by giving them very human characteristics. Choose one character and identify the mannerisms, or traits, that make him or her seem real.*

*5. The word refute means "disprove." Assuming that the title of the story is a statement made by one of the characters, tell which character would make it and why. Then explain why, in the end, the title is ironic.*

● "A Christmas Memory" is a story of love and friendship between a young boy and his elderly cousin. Truman Capote wrote the story on a hot January night in Hong Kong — far from the "frost and silence" of his childhood winters in rural Alabama. But neither the passage of time nor the separation of miles dim the cherished memory of his friend and the time they spent together.

## Truman Capote

# A CHRISTMAS MEMORY

IMAGINE A MORNING IN LATE NOVEMBER. A COM-ing of winter morning more than twenty years ago. Consider the kitchen of a spreading old house in a country town. A great black stove is its main feature; but there is also a big round table and a fireplace with two rocking chairs placed in front of it. Just today the fireplace commenced[1] its seasonal roar.

A woman with shorn white hair is standing at the kitchen window. She is wearing tennis shoes and a shapeless gray sweater over a summery calico dress. She is small and sprightly, like a bantam hen; but, due to a long youthful illness, her shoulders are pitifully hunched. Her face is remarkable — not unlike Lincoln's, craggy like that, and tinted by sun and wind; but it is delicate too, finely boned, and her eyes are sherry-colored and timid. "Oh my," she exclaims, her breath smoking the windowpane, "it's fruitcake weather!"

The person to whom she is speaking is myself. I am seven; she is sixty-something. We are cousins, very distant ones, and we have lived together — well, as long as I can remember. Other people inhabit the house, relatives; and though they have power over us, and frequently make us cry, we are not, on the whole, too much aware of them. We are each other's best friend. She calls me Buddy, in memory of a boy who was formerly her best friend. The other Buddy died in the 1880's, when she was still a child. She is still a child.

"I knew it before I got out of bed," she says, turning away from the window with a purposeful excitement in her eyes. "The court-house bell sounded so cold and clear. And there were no birds singing; they've gone to warmer country, yes indeed. Oh, Buddy, stop stuffing biscuits and fetch our buggy. Help me find my hat. We've thirty cakes to bake."

It's always the same: a morning arrives in November, and my friend, as though officially inaugurating the Christmas time of year that exhilarates her imagination and fuels the blaze of her heart, announces: "It's fruitcake weather! Fetch our buggy. Help me find my hat."

The hat is found, a straw cartwheel corsaged with velvet roses out-of-doors has faded: it once belonged to a more fashionable relative. Together, we guide our buggy, a dilapidated baby carriage, out to the garden and into a grove of pecan trees. The buggy is mine; that is, it was bought for me when I was born. It is made of wicker, rather unraveled, and the wheels wobble like a

drunkard's legs. But it is a faithful object; springtimes, we take it to the woods and fill it with flowers, herbs, wild fern for our porch pots; in the summer, we pile it with picnic paraphernalia[2] and sugar-cane fishing poles and roll it down to the edge of a creek; it has its winter uses, too: as a truck for hauling firewood from the yard to the kitchen, as a warm bed for Queenie, our tough little orange and white rat terrier who has survived distemper[3] and two rattlesnake bites. Queenie is trotting beside it now.

Three hours later we are back in the kitchen hulling a heaping buggyload of windfall pecans.[4] Our backs hurt from gathering them: how hard they were to find (the main crop having been shaken off the trees and sold by the orchard's owners, who are not us) among the concealing leaves, the frosted, deceiving grass. Caarackle! A cheery crunch, scraps of miniature thunder sound as the shells collapse and the golden mound of sweet, oily, ivory meat mounts in the milk-glass bowl. Queenie begs to taste, and now and again my friend sneaks her a mite, though insisting we deprive ourselves. "We mustn't, Buddy. If we start, we won't stop. And there's scarcely enough as there is. For thirty cakes." The kitchen is growing dark. Dusk turns the window into a mirror: our reflections mingle with the rising moon as we work by the fireside in the firelight. At last, when the moon is quite high, we toss the final hull into the fire and, with joined sighs, watch it catch flame. The buggy is empty, the bowl is brimful.

We eat our supper (cold biscuits, bacon, blackberry jam) and discuss tomorrow. Tomorrow the kind of work I like best begins: buying. Cherries and citron, ginger and vanilla and canned Hawaiian pineapple, rinds and raisins and walnuts and whiskey and oh, so much flour, butter, so many eggs, spices, flavorings: why, we'll need a pony to pull the buggy home.

But before these purchases can be made, there is the question of money. Neither of us has any. Except for skinflint sums persons in the house occasionally provide (a dime is considered very big money); or what we earn ourselves from various activities: holding rummage sales, selling buckets of handpicked blackberries, jars of homemade jam and apple jelly and peach preserves, rounding up flowers for funerals and weddings. Once we won seventy-ninth prize, five dollars, in a national football contest. Not that we know a fool thing about football. It's just that we enter any contest we hear about: at the moment our hopes are centered on the fifty-thousand-dollar Grand Prize being offered to name a new brand of coffee (we suggested "A.M."; and, after some hesitation, for my friend thought it perhaps sacrilegious, the slogan "A.M.! Amen!"). To tell the truth, our only *really* profitable enterprise was the Fun and Freak Museum we conducted in a backyard woodshed two summers ago. The Fun was a stereopticon[5] with slide views of Washington and New York lent us by a relative who had been to those places (she was furious when she discovered why we'd borrowed it); the Freak was a three-legged biddy chicken hatched by one of our own hens. Everybody hereabouts wanted to see that biddy: we charged grownups a nickel, kids two cents. And took in a good twenty dollars before the museum shut down due to the decease of the main attraction.

But one way and another we do each year accumulate Christmas savings, a Fruitcake Fund. These moneys we keep hidden in an ancient bead purse under a loose board under the floor under a chamber pot under my friend's bed. The purse is seldom removed from this safe location except to make a deposit, or, as happens every Saturday, a withdrawal; for on Saturdays I am allowed ten cents to go to the picture show. My friend has never been to a picture show, nor does she intend to: "I'd rather hear you tell the story, Buddy. That way I can imagine it more. Besides, a person my age shouldn't squander their eyes. When the Lord comes, let me see Him clear." In addition to never having seen a movie, she has never: eaten in a restaurant, traveled more than five miles from home, received or sent a telegram, read anything except funny papers and the Bible, worn cosmetics, cursed, wished someone harm, told a lie on purpose, let a hungry dog go hungry. Here are a few things she has done, does do: killed with a hoe the biggest rattlesnake ever seen in this county (sixteen rattles), dip snuff (secretly), tame hummingbirds (just try it) till they balance on her finger, tell ghost stories (we both believe in ghosts) so tingling they chill you in July, talk to herself, take walks in the rain, grow the prettiest japonicas in town, know the recipe for every sort of old-time Indian cure, including a magical wart-remover.

Now, with supper finished, we retire to the room in a faraway part of the house where my friend sleeps in a scrap-quilt-covered iron bed painted rose-pink, her favorite color. Silently, wallowing in the pleasures of conspiracy, we take the bead purse from its secret place and spill its contents on the scrap quilt. Dollar bills, tightly rolled and green as May buds. Somber fifty-cent pieces, heavy enough to weight a dead man's eyes. Lovely dimes, the liveliest coin, the one that really jingles. Nickels and quarters, worn smooth as creek pebbles. But mostly a hateful heap of bitter-odored pennies. Last summer others in the house contracted to pay us a penny for every twenty-five flies we killed. Oh, the carnage[6] of August: the flies that flew to heaven! Yet it was not work in which we took pride. And, as we sit counting pennies, it is as though we were back tabulating dead flies. Neither of us has a head for figures; we count slowly, lose track, start again. According to her calculations, we have $12.73. According to mine, exactly $13. "I do hope you're wrong, Buddy. We can't mess around with thirteen. The cakes will fall. Or put somebody in the cemetery. Why, I wouldn't dream of getting out of bed on the thirteenth." This is true: she always spends thirteenths in bed. So, to be on the safe side, we subtract a penny and toss it out the window.

Of the ingredients that go into our fruitcakes, whiskey is the most expensive, as well as the hardest to obtain: State laws forbid its sale. But everybody knows you can buy a bottle from Mr. Haha Jones. And the next day, having completed our more prosaic[7] shopping, we set out for Mr. Haha's business address, a "sinful" (to quote public opinion) fish-fry and dancing cafe down by the river. We've been there before, and on the same errand; but in previous years our dealings have been with Haha's wife, an iodine-dark Indian woman with brassy peroxided hair and a dead-tired disposition. Actually, we've never laid eyes on her husband, though we've heard that he's an Indian too. A giant with razor scars across his cheeks. They call him Haha because he's so gloomy, a man who never laughs. As we approach his cafe (a large log cabin festooned inside and out with chains of garish-gay naked lightbulbs and standing by the river's muddy edge under the shade of river trees where moss drifts through the branches like gray mist) our steps slow down. Even Queenie stops prancing and sticks close by. People have been murdered in Haha's cafe. Cut to pieces. Hit on the head. There's a case coming up in court next month. Naturally these goings-on happen at night when the colored lights cast crazy patterns and the Victrola[8] wails. In the daytime Haha's is shabby and deserted. I knock at the door, Queenie barks, my friend calls: "Mrs. Haha, ma'am? Anyone to home?"

Footsteps. The door opens. Our hearts overturn. It's Mr. Haha Jones himself! And he *is* a giant; he *does* have scars; he *doesn't* smile. No, he glowers at us through Satan-tilted eyes and demands to know: "What you want with Haha?"

For a moment we are too paralyzed to tell. Presently my friend half-finds her voice, a whispery voice at best: "If you please, Mr. Haha, we'd like a quart of your finest whiskey."

His eyes tilt more. Would you believe it? Haha is smiling! Laughing, too. "Which one of you is a drinkin' man?"

"It's for making fruitcakes, Mr. Haha. Cooking."

This sobers him. He frowns. "That's no way to waste good whiskey." Nevertheless, he retreats into the shadowed cafe and seconds later appears carrying a bottle of daisy yellow unlabeled liquor. He demonstrates its sparkle in the sunlight and says: "Two dollars."

We pay him with nickels and dimes and pennies. Suddenly, jangling the coins in his hand like a fistful of dice, his face softens. "Tell you what," he proposes, pouring the money back into our bead purse, "just send me one of them fruitcakes instead."

"Well," my friend remarks on our way home, "there's a lovely man. We'll put an extra cup of raisins in *his* cake."

The black stove, stoked with coal and firewood, glows like a lighted pumpkin. Eggbeaters whirl, spoons spin round in bowls of butter and sugar, vanilla sweetens the air, ginger spices it; melting, nose-tingling odors saturate[9] the kitchen, suffuse the house, drift out to the world on puffs of chimney smoke. In four days our work is done. Thirty-one cakes, dampened with whiskey, bask on window sills and shelves.

Who are they for?

Friends. Not necessarily neighbor friends: indeed, the larger share are intended for persons we've met maybe once, perhaps not at all. People who've struck our fancy. Like President Roosevelt. Like the Reverend and Mrs. J. C. Lucey, Baptist missionaries to Borneo, who lectured here last winter. Or the little knife grinder who comes through town twice a year. Or Abner Packer, the driver of the six o'clock bus from Mobile, who exchanges waves with us every day as he passes in a dust cloud whoosh. Or the young Wistons, a California couple whose car one afternoon broke down outside the house and who spent a pleasant hour chatting with us on the porch (young Mr. Wiston snapped our picture, the only we've ever had taken). Is it because my friend is shy with everyone *except* strangers that these strangers, and merest acquaintances, seem to us our truest friends? I think yes. Also, the scrapbooks we keep of thank-you's on White House stationery, time-to-time communications from California and Borneo, the knife grinder's penny post cards, make us feel connected to eventful worlds beyond the kitchen with its view of a sky that stops.

Now a nude December fig branch grates against the window. The kitchen is empty, the cakes are gone; yesterday we carted the last of them to the post office, where the cost of stamps turned our purse inside out. We're broke. That rather depresses me, but my friend insists on celebrating — with two inches of whiskey left in Haha's bottle. Queenie has a spoonful in a bowl of coffee (she likes her coffee chicory-flavored and strong). The rest we divide between a pair of jelly glasses. We're both quite awed at the prospect of drinking straight whiskey; the taste of it brings screwed-up expressions and sour shudders. But by and by we begin to sing, the two of us singing different songs simultaneously. I don't know the words to mine, just: *Come on along, come on along, to the dark-town strutters' ball.* But I can dance: that's what I mean to be, a tap dancer in the movies. My dancing shadow rollicks on the walls; our voices rock the chinaware; we giggle: as if unseen hands were tickling us. Queenie rolls on her back, her paws plow the air, something like a grin stretches her black lips. Inside myself, I feel warm and sparky as those crumbling logs, carefree as the wind in the chimney. My friend waltzes round the stove, the hem of her poor calico skirt pinched between her fingers as though it were a party dress: *Show me the way to go home*, she sings, her tennis shoes squeaking on the floor. *Show me the way to go home.*

Enter: two relatives. Very angry. Potent with eyes that scold, tongues that scald. Listen to what they have to say, the words tumbling together into a wrathful[10] tune. "A child of seven! whiskey on his breath! are you out of your mind? feeding a child of seven! must be loony! road to ruination! remember Cousin Kate? Uncle Charlie? Uncle Charlie's brother-in-law? shame! scandal! humiliation! kneel, pray, beg the Lord!"

Queenie sneaks under the stove. My friend gazes at her shoes, her chin quivers, she lifts her skirt and blows her nose and runs to her room. Long after the town has gone to sleep and the house is silent except for the chimings of clocks and the sputter of fading fires, she is weeping into a pillow already as wet as a widow's handkerchief.

"Don't cry," I say, sitting at the bottom of her bed and shivering despite my flannel nightgown that smells of last winter's cough syrup, "don't cry," I beg, teasing her toes, tickling her feet, "you're too old for that."

"It's because," she hiccups, "I *am* too old. Old and funny."

"Not funny. Fun. More fun than anybody. Listen. If you don't stop crying you'll be so tired tomorrow we can't go cut a tree."

She straightens up. Queenie jumps on the bed (where Queenie is not allowed) to lick her cheeks. "I know where we'll find pretty trees, Buddy. And holly, too. With berries big as your eyes. It's way off in the woods. Farther than we've ever been. Papa used to bring us Christmas trees from there: carry them on his shoulder. That's fifty years ago. Well, now: I can't wait for morning."

Morning. Frozen rime[11] lusters the grass; the sun, round as an orange and orange as hot-weather moons, balances on the horizon, burnishes the silvered winter woods. A wild turkey calls. A renegade hog grunts in the undergrowth. Soon, by the edge of knee-deep, rapid-running water, we have to abandon the buggy. Queenie wades the stream first, paddles across, barking complaints at the swiftness of the current, the pneumonia-making coldness of it. We follow, holding our shoes and equipment (a hatchet, a burlap sack) above our heads. A mile more: of chastising thorns, burrs and briers that catch our clothes; of rusty pine needles brilliant with gaudy fungus and molted feathers. Here, there, a flash, a flutter, an ecstasy of shrillings remind us that not all the birds have flown south. Always, the path unwinds through lemony sun pools and pitch pine tunnels. Another creek to cross: a disturbed armada of speckled trout froths the water round us, and frogs the size of plates practice belly flops; beaver workmen are building a dam. On the farther shore, Queenie shakes herself and trembles. My friend shivers, too: not with cold but enthusiasm. One of her hat's ragged roses sheds a petal as she lifts her head and inhales the pine-heavy air. "We're almost there; can you smell it, Buddy?" she says, as though we were approaching an ocean.

And, indeed, it is a kind of ocean. Scented acres of holiday trees, prickly-leafed holly. Red berries, shiny as Chinese bells: black crows swoop upon them screaming. Having stuffed our burlap sacks with enough greenery and crimson to garland a dozen windows, we set about choosing a tree. "It should be," muses my friend, "twice as tall as a boy. So a boy can't steal the star." The one we pick is twice as tall as me. A brave handsome brute that survives thirty hatchet strokes before it keels with a creaking, rending cry. Lugging it like a kill, we commence the long trek out. Every few yards we abandon the struggle, sit down and pant. But we have the strength of triumphant huntsmen; that and the tree's virile, icy perfume revive us, goad us on. Many compliments accompany our sunset return along the red clay road to town; but my friend is sly and noncommital when passers-by praise the treasure perched on our buggy: what a fine tree and where did it come from? "Yonderways," she murmurs vaguely. Once a car stops and the rich mill owner's lazy wife leans out and whines: "Giveya two-bits cash for that ol tree." Ordinarily my friend is afraid of saying no; but on this occasion she promptly shakes her head: "We wouldn't take a dollar." The mill owner's wife persists. "A dollar, my foot! Fifty cents. That's my last offer. Goodness, woman, you can get another one." In answer, my friend gently reflects: "I doubt it. There's never two of anything."

Home: Queenie slumps by the fire and sleeps till tomorrow, snoring loud as a human.

A trunk in the attic contains: a shoebox of ermine tails (off the opera cape of a curious lady who once rented a room in the house), coils of frazzled tinsel gone gold with age, one silver star, a brief rope of dilapidated, undoubtedly dangerous candy-like light bulbs. Excellent decorations, as far as they go, which isn't far enough: my friend wants our tree to blaze "like a Baptist window," droop with weighty snows of ornament. But we can't afford the made-in-Japan splendors at the five-and-dime. So we do what we've always done: sit for days at the kitchen table with scissors and crayons and stacks of colored paper. I make sketches and my friend cuts them out: lots of cats, fish too (because they're easy to draw), some apples, some watermelons, a few winged angels devised from saved-up sheets of Hershey-bar tin foil. We use safety pins to attach these creations to the tree; as a final touch, we sprinkle the branches with shredded cotton (picked in August for this purpose). My friend, surveying the effect, clasps her hands together. "Now honest, Buddy. Doesn't it look good enough to eat?" Queenie tries to eat an angel.

After weaving and ribboning holly wreaths for all the front windows, our next project is the fashioning of family gifts. Tie-dye scarves for the ladies, for the men a home-brewed lemon and licorice and aspirin syrup to be taken "at the first Symptoms of a Cold and after Hunting." But when it comes time for making each other's gift, my friend and I separate to work secretly. I would like to buy her a pearl-handled knife, a radio, a whole pound of chocolate-covered cherries (we tasted some once, and she always swears: "I could live on them, Buddy, Lord yes I could — and that's not taking His name in vain"). Instead, I am building her a kite. She would like to give me a bicycle (she's said so on several million occasions: "If only I could, Buddy. It's bad enough in life to do without something *you* want; but confound it, what gets my goat is not being able to give somebody something you want *them* to have. Only one of these days I will, Buddy. Locate you a bike. Don't ask how. Steal it, maybe"). Instead, I'm fairly certain that she is building me a kite — the same as last year, and the year before: the year before that we exchanged slingshots. All of which is fine by me. For we are champion kite-fliers who study the wind like sailors; my friend, more accomplished than I, can get a kite aloft when there isn't enough breeze to carry clouds.

Christmas Eve afternoon we scrape together a nickel and go to the butcher's to buy Queenie's traditional gift, a good gnawable beef bone. The bone, wrapped in funny paper, is placed high in the tree near the silver star. Queenie knows it's there. She squats at the foot of the tree staring up in a trance of greed: when bedtime arrives she refuses to budge. Her excitement is equaled by my own. I kick the covers and turn my pillow as though it were a scorching summer's night. Somewhere a rooster crows: falsely, for the sun is still on the other side of the world.

"Buddy, are you awake?" It is my friend, calling from her room, which is next to mine; and an instant later she is sitting on my bed holding a candle. "Well, I can't sleep a hoot," she declares. "My mind's jumping like a jack rabbit. Buddy, do you think Mrs. Roosevelt will serve our cake at dinner?" We huddle in the bed, and she squeezes my hand I-love-you. "Seems like your hand used to be so much smaller. I guess I hate to see you grow up. When you're grown up, will we still be friends?" I say always. "But I feel so bad, Buddy. I wanted so bad to give you a bike. I tried to sell my cameo Papa gave me. Buddy" — she hesitates, as though embarrassed — "I made you another kite." Then I confess that I made her one, too; and we laugh. The candle burns too short to hold. Out it goes, exposing the starlight, the stars spinning at the window like a visible caroling that slowly, slowly daybreak silences. Possibly we doze; but the beginnings of dawn splash us like cold water: we're up, wide-eyed and wandering while we wait for others to waken. Quite deliberately my friend drops a kettle on the kitchen floor. I tap-dance in front of closed doors. One by one the household emerges, looking as though they'd like to kill us both; but it's Christmas, so they can't. First, a gorgeous breakfast:

just everything you can imagine — from flapjacks and fried squirrel to hominy grits and honey-in-the-comb. Which puts everyone in a good humor except my friend and I. Frankly, we're so impatient to get at the presents we can't eat a mouthful.

Well, I'm disappointed. Who wouldn't be? With socks, a Sunday school shirt, some handkerchiefs, a hand-me-down sweater and a year's subscription to a religious magazine for children. *The Little Shepherd*. It makes me boil. It really does.

My friend has a better haul. A sack of Satsumas,[12] that's her best present. She is proudest, however, of a white wool shawl knitted by her married sister. But she *says* her favorite gift is the kite I built her. And it *is* very beautiful; though not as beautiful as the one she made me, which is blue and scattered with gold and green Good Conduct stars; moreover, my name is painted on it, "Buddy."

"Buddy, the wind is blowing."

The wind is blowing, and nothing will do till we've run to a pasture below the house where Queenie has scooted to bury her bone (and where, a winter hence, Queenie will be buried, too). There, plunging through the healthy waist-high grass, we unreel our kites, feel them twitching at the string—like sky fish as they swim into the wind. Satisfied, sun-warmed, we sprawl in the grass and peel Satsumas and watch our kites cavort. Soon I forget the socks and hand-me-down sweater. I'm as happy as if we'd already won the fifty-thousand-dollar Grand Prize in that coffee-naming contest.

"My, how foolish I am!" my friend cries, suddenly alert, like a woman remembering too late she has biscuits in the oven. "You know what I've always thought?" she asks in a tone of discovery, and not smiling at me but a point beyond. "I've always thought a body would have to be sick and dying before they saw the Lord. And I imagined that when He came it would be like looking at the Baptist window: pretty as colored glass with the sun pouring through, such a shine you don't know it's getting dark. And it's been a comfort: to think of that shine taking away all the spooky feeling. But I'll wager it never happens. I'll wager at the very end a body realizes the Lord has already shown Himself. That things as they are" — her hand circles in a gesture that gathers clouds and kites and grass and Queenie pawing earth over her bone — "just what they've always been, was seeing Him. As for me, I could leave the world with today in my eyes."

This is our last Christmas together.

Life separates us. Those who Know Best decide that I belong in a military school. And so follows a miserable succession of bugle-blowing prisons, grim reveille-ridden summer camps. I have a new home too. But it doesn't count. Home is where my friend is, and there I never go.

And there she remains, puttering around the kitchen. Alone with Queenie. Then alone. ("Buddy dear," she writes in her wild hard-to-read script, "yesterday Jim Macy's horse kicked Queenie bad. Be thankful she didn't feel much. I wrapped her in a Fine Linen sheet and rode her in the buggy down to Simpson's pasture where she can be with all her Bones. . . .") For a few Novembers she continues to bake her fruitcakes single-handed; not as many, but some: and, of course, she always sends me "the best of the batch." Also, in every letter she encloses a dime wadded in toilet paper: "See a picture show and write me the story." But gradually in her letters she tends to confuse me with her other friend, the Buddy who died in the 1880's; more and more thirteenths are not the only days she stays in bed: a morning arrives in November, a leafless birdless coming of winter morning, when she cannot rouse herself to exclaim: "Oh my, it's fruitcake weather!"

And when that happens, I know it. A message saying so merely confirms a piece of news some secret vein had already received, severing[13] from me an irreplaceable part of myself, letting it loose like a kite on a broken string. That is why, walking around a school campus on this particular December morning, I keep searching the sky. As if I expected to see, rather like hearts, a lost pair of kites hurrying toward heaven.

[1] **commenced:** began
[2] **paraphernalia:** equipment
[3] **distemper:** a serious disease of dogs and other animals
[4] **windfall pecans:** nuts blown down from trees by the wind
[5] **stereopticon:** projector for slides with a double image
[6] **carnage:** great and bloody slaughter
[7] **prosaic:** commonplace; ordinary
[8] **Victrola:** record player
[9] **saturate:** spread throughout; fill full
[10] **wrathful:** very angry
[11] **rime:** white frost
[12] **Satsumas:** a type of orange
[13] **severing:** cutting or breaking off from a whole

## A CLOSER LOOK

*1. Buddy's cousin is not very highly regarded by the family. Why do you think this is so?*

*2. Buddy says that the relatives who live in the house have power over him and his cousin and "frequently make us cry." Find an example in the story that illustrates this. How do you think the way they are treated by the rest of the family affects the way Buddy and his friend feel about each other?*

*3. Buddy's cousin lived and died within a five mile area. Her activities were limited. Was her outlook on life limited? Explain your answer.*

*4. Think about the discovery that Buddy's friend makes while she and Buddy are flying kites on their last Christmas day together. Then explain why she says, "I could leave the world with today in my eyes."*

*5. The message confirming his friend's death severs from Buddy an "irreplaceable" part of himself. Who — or what — is that irreplaceable part? Why does he search the sky, expecting to see "a lost pair of kites hurrying toward heaven"? What do the kites symbolize, or represent, in the story?*

● The circus is the battleground. Harriet and the Fly family are the contenders. Harriet prides herself on having nerves of steel. The Fly family prides itself on terrifying the audience with death-defying acts high in the air. Harriet refuses to be terrified. It's a battle of nerves. Who is going to win?

## Toni Cade Bambara

# MY DELICATE HEART CONDITION

**M**Y COUSIN JOANNE HAS NOT BEEN ALLOWED to hang out with me for some time because she went and told Aunt Hazel that I scare her to death whenever she sleeps over at our house or I spend the weekend at hers. The truth is I sometimes like to tell stories about blood-thirsty vampires or ugly monsters that lurk in clothes closets or giant beetles that eat their way through the shower curtain, like I used to do at camp to entertain the kids in my bunk. But Joanne always cries and that makes the stories even weirder, like background music her crying. And too — I'm not going to lie about it — I get spookier on purpose until all the little crybabies are stuffing themselves under their pillows and throwing their sneakers at me and making such a racket that Mary the counselor has to come in and shine her flashlight around the bunkhouse. I play like I'm asleep. The rest of them are too busy blubbering and finding their way out from under the blankets to tell Mary that it's me. Besides, once they get a load of her standing against the moonlight in that long white robe of hers looking like a ghost, they just start up again and pretty soon the whole camp is awake. Anyway, that's what I do for fun. So Joanne hasn't been around. And this year I'll have to go to the circus by myself and to camp without her. My mother said on the phone to Aunt Hazel — "Good, keep Jo over there and maybe Harriet'll behave herself if she's got no one to show off to." For all the years my mother's known me, she still doesn't understand that my behaving has got nothing to do with who I hang out with. A private thing between

151

me and me or maybe between me and the Fly family since they were the ones that first got me to sit through monster movies and withstand all the terror I could take.

For four summers now, me and the Fly family have had this thing going. A battle of nerves, you might say. Each year they raise the rope closer and closer to the very top of the tent — I hear they're going to perform outdoors this year and be even higher — and they stretch the rope further across the rings where the clowns and the pony riders perform. Each year they get bolder and more daring with their rope dancing and the swinging by the legs and flinging themselves into empty space making everyone throw

up their hands and gasp for air until Mr. Fly at the very last possible second swings out on his bar to catch them up by the tips of their heels. Everyone just dies and clutches at their hearts. Everybody but me. I sit there calmly. I've trained myself. Joanne used to die and duck her head under the benches and stay there till it was all over.

Last summer they really got bold. On the final performance just before the fair closed, and some revival type tent show[1] comes in and all the kids go off to camp, the Fly family performed without a net. I figured they'd be up to something so I made sure my stomach was like steel. I did ten push-ups before breakfast, twenty sit-ups before lunch, skipped dinner altogether. My brother Teddy kidded me all day — "Harriet's trying out for the Olympics." I passed up the icie man on the corner and the pizza and sausage stand by the schoolyard and the cotton candy and jelly apple lady and the pickle and penny candy boy, in fact I passed up all the stands that lead from the street down the little roadway to the fair grounds that used to be a swamp when we first moved from Baltimore to Jamaica, Long Island. It wasn't easy, I'm not going to lie, but I was taking no chances. Between the balloon man and the wheel of fortune was the usual clump of ladies from church who came night after night to try to win the giant punch bowl set on the top shelf above the wheel, but had to settle night after night for a jar of gumdrops or salt and pepper shakers or some other little thing from the bottom shelf. And from the wheel of fortune to the tent was at least a million stands selling B.B. bats and jawbreakers and gingerbread and sweet potato pie and frozen custard and — like I said it wasn't easy. A million ways to tempt you, to unsettle your stomach, and make you lose the battle to the Fly family.

I sat there almost enjoying the silly clowns who came tumbling out of a steamer trunk no bigger than the one we have in the basement where my mother keeps my old report cards and photographs and letters and things. And I almost enjoyed the fire eater and the knife thrower, but I was so close up I could see how there wasn't any real thrill. I almost enjoyed the fat-leg girls who rode the ponies two at a time and standing up, but their costumes weren't very pretty — just an ordinary polo shirt like you get if you run in the PAL[2] meets and short skirts you can wear on either side like the big girls wear at the roller rink. And I almost enjoyed the jugglers except that my Uncle Bubba can juggle the dinner plates better any day of the week so long as Aunt Hazel isn't there to stop him. I was impatient and started yawning. Finally all the clowns hitched up their baggy pants and tumbled over each other out of the ring and into the dark, the jugglers caught all the things that were up in the air and yawning just like me went off to the side. The pony girls brought their horses to a sudden stop that raised a lot of dust, then jumped down into the dirt and bowed. Then the ringmaster stepped into the circle of light and tipped his hat which was a little raggedy from where I was sitting and said — "And now, Ladieeez and Gentlemen, what you've alll been waiting forrr, the Main aTTRACtion, the FLY FAMILEEE." And everyone jumped up to shout like crazy as they came running out on their toes to stand in the light and then climb the ropes. I took a deep breath and folded my arms over my chest and a kid next to me went into hiding, acting like she was going to tie her shoelaces.

There used to be four of them — the father, a big guy with a bald head and a bushy mustache and shoulders and arms like King Kong; a tall lanky mother whom you'd never guess could even climb into a high chair or catch anything heavier than a Ping-Pong ball to look at her; the oldest son who looked like his father except he had hair on his head but none on his face and a big face it was, so that no matter how high up he got you could always tell whether he was smiling or frowning or counting; the younger boy about thirteen, maybe, had a vacant stare like he was a million miles away feeding his turtles or something, anything but walking along a tightrope or flying through the air with his family. I had always liked to watch him because he was as cool as I was. But last summer the little girl got into the act. My grandmother says she's probably a midget 'cause no self-respecting mother would allow her child to be up there acting like a bird. "Just a baby," she'd say. "Can't be more than six years old. Should be home in bed. Must be a midget." My grandfather would give me a look when she started in and we'd smile at her together.

They almost got to me that last performance, dodging around with new routines and two at a time so that you didn't know which one Mr. Fly was going to save at the last minute. But he'd fly out and catch the little boy and swing over to the opposite stand where the big boy was flying out to catch them both by the wrists and the poor woman would be left kind of dangling there, suspended, then she'd do this double flip which would kill off everyone in the tent except me, of course, and swing out on the very bar she was on in the first place. And then they'd mess around two or three flying at once just to confuse you until the big drum roll started and out steps the little girl in a party dress and a huge blindfold wrapped around her little head and a pink umbrella like they sell down in Chinatown. And I almost — I won't lie about it — I almost let my heart thump me off the bench. I almost thought I too had to tie my shoelaces. But I sat there. Stubborn. And the kid starts bouncing up and down on the rope like she was about to take off and tear through the canvas roof. Then out swings her little brother and before you know it, Fly Jr. like a great eagle with his arms flapping grabs up the kid, her eyeband in his teeth and swoops her off to the bar that's already got Mrs. Mr. and Big Bro on it and surely there's no room for him. And everyone's standing on their feet clutching at their faces. Everyone but me. 'Cause I know from the getgo[3] that Mr. and Mrs. are going to leave the bar to give Jr. room and fly over to the other side. Which is exactly what they do. The lady in front of me, Mrs. Perez, who does all the sewing in our neighborhood, gets up and starts shaking her hands like ladies do to get the fingernail polish dry and she says to me with her eyes jammed shut "I must go finish the wedding gowns. Tell me later who died." And she scoots through the aisle, falling all over everybody with her eyes still shut and never looks up. And Mrs. Caine taps me on the back and leans over and says, "Some people just can't take it." And I smile at her and at her twins who're sitting there with their mouths open. I fold my arms over my chest and just dare the Fly family to do their very worst.

The minute I got to camp, I ran up to the main house where all the counselors gather to say hello to the parents and talk with the directors. I had to tell Mary the latest doings with the Fly family. But she put a finger to her mouth like she sometimes does to shush me. "Let's not have any scary stuff this summer, Harriet," she said, looking over my shoulder at a new kid. This new kid, Willie, was from my old neighborhood in Baltimore so we got friendly right off. Then he told me that he had a romantic heart so I quite naturally took him under my wing and decided not to give him a heart attack with any ghost tales. Mary said he meant "rheumatic"[4] heart, but I don't see any difference. So I told Mary to move him out of George's tent and give him a nicer counselor who'd respect his romantic heart. George used to be my play boyfriend when I first came to camp as a little kid and didn't know any better. But he's not a nice person. He makes up funny nicknames for people which aren't funny at all. Like calling Eddie Michaels the Watermelon Kid or David Farmer Charcoal Plenty which I really do not appreciate and especially from a counselor. And once he asked Joanne, who was the table monitor, to go fetch a pail of milk from the kitchen. And the minute she got up, he started hatching a plot, trying to get the kids to hide her peanut butter sandwich and put spiders in her soup. I had to remind everyone at the table that Joanne was my first cousin by blood, and I would be forced to waste the first bum that laid a hand on her plate. And ole George says, "Oh don't be a dumbhead, Harriet. Jo's so stupid she won't even notice." And I told him right then and there that I was not his play girlfriend anymore and would rather marry the wolfman than grow up and be his wife. And just in case he didn't get the message, that night around campfire when we were all playing Little Sally Walker sittin' in a saucer and it was my turn to shake it to the east and to shake it to the west and to shake it to the very one that I loved the best — I shook straight for Mr. Nelson the lifeguard, who was not only the ugliest person in camp but the archenemy of ole George.

And that very first day of camp last summer when Willie came running up to me to get in line for lunch, here comes George talking some simple stuff about "What a beautiful head you have, Willie. A long, smooth, streamlined head. A sure sign of superior gifts. Definitely genius proportions." And poor Willie went for it, grinning and carrying on and touching his head, which if you want to know the truth is a bullet head and that's all there is to it. And he's turning to me every which way, like he's modeling his head in a fashion show. And the minute his back is turned, ole George makes a face about Willie's head and all the kids in the line bust out laughing. So I had to beat up a few right then and there and finish off the rest later in the shower for being so stupid, laughing at a kid with a romantic heart.

One night in the last week of August when the big campfire party is held, it was very dark and the moon was all smoky, and I just couldn't help myself and started in with a story about the great caterpillar who was going to prowl through the tents and nibble off everybody's toes. And Willie started this whimpering in the back of his throat so I had to switch the story real quick to something cheerful. But before I could do that, ole George picked up my story and added a wicked witch who put spells on city kids who come to camp, and a hunchback dwarf that chopped up tents and bunk beds, and a one-eyed phantom giant who gobbled up the hearts of underprivileged kids. And every time he got to the part where the phantom ripped out a heart, poor Willie would get louder and louder until finally he started rolling around in the grass and screaming and all the kids went crazy and scattered behind the rocks almost kicking the fire completely out as they dashed off into the darkness yelling bloody murder. And the counselors could hardly round us all up — me, too, I'm not going to lie about it. Their little circles of flashlight bobbing in and out of the bushes along the patches of pine, bumping into each other as they scrambled for us kids. And poor Willie rolling

157

around something awful, so they took him to the infirmary.

I was sneaking some gingersnaps in to him later that night when I hear Mary and another senior counselor fussing at ole George in the hallway.

"You've been picking on that kid ever since he got here, George. But tonight was the limit — "

"I wasn't picking on him, I was just trying to tell a story — "

"All that talk about hearts, gobblin' up hearts and underpriv — "

"Yeh, you were directing it all at the little kid. You should be — "

"I wasn't talking about him. They're all underprivileged kids, after all. I mean all the kids are underprivileged."

I huddled back into the shadows and almost banged into Willie's iron bed. I was hoping he'd open his eyes and wink at me and tell me he was just fooling. That it wasn't so bad to have an underprivileged heart. But he just slept. "I'm an underprivileged kid too," I thought to myself. I knew it was a special camp, but I'd never realized. No wonder Aunt Hazel screamed so about my scary stories and my mother flicked off the TV when the monsters came on and Mary was always shushing me. We all had bad hearts. I crawled into the supply cabinet to wait for Willie to wake up so I could ask him about it all. I ate all the gingersnaps but I didn't feel any better. You have a romantic heart, I whispered to myself settling down among the bandages. You will have to be very careful.

It didn't make any difference to Aunt Hazel that I had changed, that I no longer told scary stories or dragged my schoolmates to the latest creature movie, or raced my friends to the edge of the roof, or held my breath, or ran under the train rail when the train was already in sight. As far as she was concerned, I was still the same ole spooky kid I'd always been. So Joanne was kept at home. My mother noticed the difference, but she said over the phone to my grandmother, "She's acting very ladylike these days, growing up." I didn't tell her about my secret, that I knew about my heart. And I was kind of glad Joanne wasn't around 'cause I would have blabbed it all to her and scared her to death. When school starts again, I decided, I'll ask my teacher how to outgrow my underprivileged heart. I'll train myself, just like I did with the Fly family.

"Well, I guess you'll want some change to go to the fair again, hunh?" my mother said coming into my room dumping things in her pocketbook.

"No," I said. "I'm too grown up for circuses."

She put the money on the dresser anyway. I was lying, of course. I was thinking what a terrible strain it would be for Mrs. Perez and everybody else if while sitting there, with the Fly family zooming around in the open air a million miles above the ground, little Harriet Watkins should drop dead with a fatal heart attack behind them.

"I lost," I said out loud.

"Lost what?"

"The battle with the Fly family."

She just stood there a long time looking at me, trying to figure me out, the way mothers are always doing but should know better. Then she kissed me good-bye and left for work.

[1] **revival type tent show:** religious services conducted by a traveling evangelist or minister

[2] **PAL:** Police Athletic League, an organization in New York City that sponsors activities for children

[3] **getgo:** beginning (slang)

[4] **rheumatic:** a condition causing inflammation of the heart valves

## A CLOSER LOOK

*1. What is the "battle of nerves" that Harriet has with the Fly family? How does she prepare herself for this battle?*

*2. Explain why Harriet takes Willie "under her wing" at camp and decides not to tell him scary stories.*

*3. Why does Harriet say that George is not a nice person? Do you agree with her opinion of him? Explain.*

*4. Why does Harriet conclude that she has a "delicate heart condition" when she overhears George say that all the campers are underprivileged?*

*5. How does Harriet's behavior change after she finds out about her "heart condition"? Why does she tell her mother that she is too grown up for circuses? Explain what she means when she says she lost the battle with the Fly family.*

*6. Though Harriet has lost one battle, we feel sure that she will go on to win many others. What qualities does she have that make us think of her as a "winner"?*

● You probably know the old story about the man who, after being bawled out by his boss, goes home and kicks his dog. The story illustrates a very human characteristic: the tendency to take out our own unhappy feelings on others. It's a tendency that none of us are proud of, but that most of us give way to from time to time. The ability to deal with disappointment *without* taking it out on others is considered a mark of maturity. Often, we attain that maturity through painful experience.

## Carson McCullers

# SUCKER

T WAS ALWAYS LIKE I HAD A ROOM TO MYSELF. Sucker slept in my bed with me but that didn't interfere with anything. The room was mine and I used it as I wanted to. Once I remember sawing a trap door in the floor. Last year when I was a sophomore in high school I tacked some pictures of girls on the walls. My mother never bothered me because she had the younger kids to look after. And Sucker thought anything I did was always swell.

Whenever I'd bring any of my friends back to my room all I had to do was just glance once at Sucker and he'd get up from whatever he was busy with and maybe half smile at me, and leave without saying a word. He never brought kids back here. He's twelve, four years younger than I am, and he always knew without me even telling him that I didn't want kids that age meddling with my things.

Half the time I used to forget that Sucker isn't my brother. He's my first cousin, but practically ever since I can remember he's been in our family. You see, his folks were killed in a wreck when he was a baby. To me and my kid sisters he was like our brother.

Sucker used to remember and believe every word I said. That's how he got his nickname. Once a couple of years ago I told him that if he'd jump off our garage with an umbrella it would act as a parachute and he wouldn't fall hard. He did it and busted his knee. That's just one instance. And the funny thing was that no matter how many times he got fooled he would still believe me. Not that

160

he was dumb in other ways — it was just the way he acted with me.

There is one thing I have learned, but it makes me feel guilty and is hard to figure out. If a person admires you a lot, you despise him and don't care — and it is the person who doesn't notice you that you are apt to admire. This is not easy to realize.

Maybelle Watts, this senior at school, acted like she was the Queen of Sheba. Yet at the same time I would have done anything in the world to get her attention. When Sucker was a little kid and on up until the time he was twelve, I guess I treated him as bad as Maybelle did me.

Now that Sucker has changed so much it is a little hard to remember him as he used to be. I never imagined I'd want to think back and compare and try to get things straight in my mind. If I could have seen ahead, maybe I would have acted different.

I never noticed him much, and when you consider how long we have had the same room together it is funny the few things I remember. He used to talk to himself a lot when he'd think he was alone — all about him fighting gangsters and being on ranches and that sort of kid stuff. Usually, though, he was very quiet. He didn't have many boys in the neighborhood to buddy with, and his face had the look of a kid who is watching a game and waiting to be asked to play. That is how I remember him — getting a little bigger every year, but still being the same. That was Sucker up until a few months ago, when all this trouble began.

Maybelle was somehow mixed up in what happened, so I guess I ought to start with her. Until I knew her I hadn't given much time to girls. Last fall she sat next to me in General Science class and that was when I first began to notice her. Her hair is the brightest yellow I ever saw and sometimes she wears it set into curls with some sort of gluey stuff. Her fingernails are pointed and painted a shiny red. All during class I used to watch Maybelle, except when I thought she was going to look my way or when the teacher called on me. Her hands are very little and white except for that red stuff, and when she would turn the pages of her book she always licked her thumb and held out her little finger and turned very slowly.

It is impossible to describe Maybelle. All the boys are crazy about her, but she didn't even notice me. For one thing she's almost two years older than I am. Between periods I used to try and pass very close to her in the halls, but she would hardly ever smile at me.

Even at night I would think about Maybelle. Sometimes Sucker
would wake up and ask me why I couldn't get settled and I'd tell
him to hush his mouth. I guess I wanted to ignore somebody like
Maybelle did me. You could always tell by Sucker's face when his
feelings were hurt. I don't remember all the ugly remarks I must
have made, because even when I was saying them my mind was on
Maybelle.

162

That went on for nearly three months and then somehow she began to change. In the halls she would speak to me and every morning she copied my homework. Then one lunchtime I danced with her in the gym, and knew everything was going to change.

It was that night when this trouble really started. I had come into my room late and Sucker was already asleep. I felt happy and keyed up and was awake thinking about Maybelle a long time. Then I dreamed about her and it seemed I kissed her. It was a surprise to wake up and see the dark. The house was quiet, and Sucker's voice was a shock.

"Pete? . . ." I didn't answer anything or even move.

"You do like me as if I was your own brother, don't you, Pete?"

I couldn't get over the surprise, and it was like this was the real dream instead of the other.

"You have liked me all the time like I was your own brother, haven't you?"

"Sure," I said.

Sucker felt little and warm against my back, and his warm breath touched my shoulder.

"No matter what you did I always knew you liked me."

I was wide awake and my mind seemed mixed up in a strange way. I guess you understand people better when you are happy than when something is worrying you. It was like I had never really thought about Sucker until then. I felt I had always been mean to him. One night a few weeks before I had heard him crying in the dark. He said he had lost a boy's beebee gun and was scared to let anybody know. He wanted me to tell him what to do. I was sleepy and tried to make him hush and when he wouldn't I kicked at him. That was just one of the things I remembered.

"You're a swell kid, Sucker," I said.

It seemed to me suddenly that I did like him more than anybody else I knew — more than any other boy, more than my sisters, more in a certain way even than Maybelle. I felt good all over and it was like when they play sad music in the movies. I wanted to show Sucker how much I really thought of him and make up for the way I had always treated him.

We talked for a good while that night. His voice was fast and it was like he had been saving up these things to tell me for a long time. He mentioned that he was going to try to build a canoe and that the kids down the block wouldn't let him in on their football team and I don't know what all. I talked some too, and it was a good feeling to think of him taking in everything I said so seriously. I even spoke of Maybelle a little, only I made out like it was her who had been running after me all this time. He asked questions about high school and so forth. His voice was excited and he kept on talking fast like he could never get the words out in time. When I went to sleep he was still talking.

During the next couple of weeks I saw a lot of Maybelle. She acted as though she really cared for me a little. Half the time I felt so good I hardly knew what to do with myself.

But I didn't forget about Sucker. There were a lot of old things in my bureau drawer I'd been saving — boxing gloves and second-rate fishing tackle. All this I turned over to him. We had some more talks and it was really like I was knowing him for the first time. When there was a long cut on his cheek I knew he had been monkeying around with this new razor set of mine, but I didn't say anything.

His face seemed different now. He used to look timid and sort of like he was afraid of a whack over the head. That expression was gone. His face, with those wide-open eyes and his ears sticking out and his mouth never quite shut, had the look of a person who is surprised and expecting something swell.

Once I started to point him out to Maybelle and tell her he was my kid brother. It was an afternoon when a murder mystery was on at the movie. I had earned a dollar working for my dad and I gave Sucker a quarter to go and get candy and so forth. With the rest I took Maybelle. We were sitting near the back and I saw Sucker come in. He began to stare at the screen the minute he stepped past the ticket man and he stumbled down the aisle without noticing where he was going. I started to punch Maybelle, but Sucker looked a little silly — walking with his eyes glued to the movie and wiping his reading glasses on his shirttail. He went on until he got to the first few rows where the kids usually sit. It felt good to have both of them at the movie with the money I earned.

I guess things went on like this for about a month or six weeks, with me feeling so good I couldn't settle down to study or put my mind on anything. I wanted to be friendly with everybody. There were times when I just had to talk to some person. And usually that would be Sucker. He felt as good as I did. Once he said: "Pete, I am glad you are like my brother. It makes me gladder than anything else in the world."

Then something happened between Maybelle and me. I never

have figured out just what it was. She began to act different. At first I tried to think it was just my imagination, but she didn't act glad to see me anymore. I'd see her out riding with this fellow on the football team who has a yellow car the color of her hair. After school she would ride off with him, laughing and looking into his face.

I couldn't think of anything to do about it and she was on my mind all day and night. When I did get a chance to go out with her she was snippy and didn't seem to notice me. This made me feel like something was the matter — I'd worry about my shoes clopping too loud on the floor or the bumps on my chin.

At first I was so worried I just forgot about Sucker. Then later he began to get on my nerves. He was always hanging around until I would get back from high school, with his waiting expression on his face. Then I wouldn't say anything or I'd maybe answer him rough-like and he would finally go out.

I can't divide that time up and say this happened one day and that the next. For one thing, I was so mixed up the weeks just slid along into each other. Maybelle still rode around with this fellow and sometimes she would smile at me and sometimes not. Every afternoon I went from one place to another where I thought she'd be.

Sucker kept getting on my nerves more and more. He looked as though he sort of blamed me for something, but at the same time knew that it wouldn't last long. He was growing fast and for some reason began to stutter. Sometimes he had nightmares or would lose his breakfast. Mom got him a bottle of cod-liver oil.

Then the finish came between Maybelle and me. I met her going to the drugstore and asked for a date. When she said no, I said something sarcastic. She told me she was sick and tired of my being around and that she had never cared a rap about me. I just stood there and didn't answer anything. I walked home slowly.

For several afternoons I stayed in my room by myself. I didn't want to go anywhere or talk to anyone. When Sucker would come in and look at me sort of funny I'd yell at him to get out. I didn't want to think of Maybelle and I sat at my desk reading or whittling at a toothbrush rack I was making. It seemed to me I was putting that girl out of my mind pretty well.

But you can't help what happens to you at night. That is what made things how they are now.

You see, I dreamed about Maybelle again. It was like the first time and Sucker woke up. He reached for my hand.

"Pete, what's the matter with you?"

All of a sudden I felt so mad my throat choked — at myself and the dream and Maybelle and Sucker and every single person I knew. I remembered all the times Maybelle had humiliated me and everything bad that ever happened. It was as if nobody would ever like me but a sap like Sucker.

"Why is it we aren't buddies like we were before? Why — ?"

"Shut your trap!" I jumped up and turned on the light. He sat in the middle of the bed, his eyes blinking and scared.

There was something in me and I couldn't help myself. I don't think anybody ever gets that mad but once. Words came without me knowing what they would be. It was only afterward that I remembered each thing I said.

"Why aren't we buddies? Because you're the dumbest slob I ever saw! Nobody cares anything about you! And just because I felt sorry for you sometimes and tried to act decent, don't think I gave a darn for a dumb little creep like you!"

If I'd talked loud or hit him it wouldn't have been so bad. But my voice was slow and like I was very calm. Sucker's mouth was partway open and he looked as though he'd knocked his funny bone. His face was white and sweat came out on his forehead. He wiped it away with the back of his hand and for a minute his arm stayed raised that way as if holding something away from him.

"Don't you know a single thing? Haven't you ever been around at all? Why don't you get a girl friend instead of me? What kind of a sissy do you want to grow up to be, anyway?"

I didn't know what was coming next. I couldn't help myself or think. Sucker didn't move. He had on one of my pajama jackets and his neck stuck out skinny and small. His hair was damp on his forehead.

"Why do you always hang around me? Don't you know when you're not wanted?"

Afterward I could remember the change in Sucker's face. Slowly that blank look went away and he closed his mouth. His eyes got narrow and his fists shut. I'd never seen such a look on him before. It was like every second he was getting older — a hard look to his eyes that seemed wrong in a kid. A drop of sweat rolled down his chin and he didn't notice. He just sat with those eyes on me and didn't speak and his face didn't move.

"No, you don't know when you're not wanted. You're too dumb, just like your name — a dumb Sucker."

It was like something had busted inside me. I turned off the lights and sat down by the window. My legs were shaking and I was so tired I could have bawled. I sat there a long time. After a while I heard Sucker lie down.

I wasn't mad anymore, only tired. It seemed awful to me that I had talked like that to a kid only twelve. I couldn't take it all in. I told myself I would go over to him and try to make it up. But I just sat there in the cold. I planned how I could straighten it out in the morning. Then, trying not to squeak the springs, I got back in bed.

Sucker was gone when I woke up the next day. And later, when I wanted to apologize as I had planned, he looked at me in this new hard way so that I couldn't say a word.

All of that was two or three months ago. Since then Sucker has grown faster than anybody I ever saw. He's almost as tall as I am and his bones have gotten heavier and bigger. He won't wear my old clothes anymore.

Our room isn't mine at all now. He's gotten up this gang of kids and they have a club. When they aren't digging trenches in some vacant lot and fighting, they are always in my room. They've rigged up a radio and every afternoon it blares out music.

It's even worse when we are alone together in the room. He sprawls across the bed and just stares at me with that hard, half-sneering look. I fiddle around my desk and can't get settled. The thing is, I have to study because I've gotten three bad cards this term already. If I flunk English I can't graduate next year. I don't want to be a bum and I just have to get my mind on it.

I don't care a flip for Maybelle anymore, and it's only this thing between Sucker and me that is the trouble now. We never speak except when we have to before the family. I don't even want to call him Sucker anymore, and unless I forget I call him by his real name, Richard. At night I can't study with him in the room and I have to hang around the drugstore with fellows who loaf there.

More than anything I want to be easy in my mind again. And I miss the way Sucker and I were for a while in a funny, sad way that before this I never would have believed. But everything is so different that there seems to be nothing I can do to get it right. I've sometimes thought if we could have it out in a big fight that would help. But I can't fight him because he's four years younger. And another thing — sometimes this look in his eyes makes me almost believe that if Sucker could, he would kill me.

## A CLOSER LOOK

*1. Pete says, "If a person admires you a lot, you despise him and don't care. . . ." We know that Pete feels this way about Sucker. Why does that make Pete feel guilty?*

*2. Pete also says that when you're happy, you understand other people better. He then goes on to back up his statement with evidence. What is that evidence?*

*3. Think about how Pete treated Sucker before, during, and after the time he was dating Maybelle. How did Pete's treatment of Sucker parallel Maybelle's treatment of him?*

*4. As the narrator, Pete tells us how he lashed out at Sucker on the night everything changed between them. Notice that Pete says he recognized his cruelty but couldn't stop himself from inflicting it on Sucker. Suppose Sucker were telling the story from his point of view. Would he have said, "Pete* couldn't *stop," or, "Pete* wouldn't *stop"? Explain.*

*5. After being mistreated for so long, Sucker finally felt he had the brotherly affection that he'd always longed for. What made him feel this way? What expectations did this feeling raise in him?*

*6. Why do you think Sucker accepted Pete's mistreatment meekly and without resentment in the past? Why doesn't he accept it now? Why, instead, does he react so violently?*

• Long before stories were written down, they were told aloud, and Indian stories are among the oldest in the world. The art of storytelling, passed along from one generation to the next, became the art of storywriting, and one of its masters is Gaurishanker Goverdhanram Joshi, who wrote under the pen name Dhumektu. "The Letter" is a story of two fathers, of faith, and love, and finally, of compassion.

## Dhumektu

# THE LETTER

IN THE GRAY SKY OF EARLY DAWN STARS STILL glowed, as happy memories light up a life that is nearing its close. An old man was walking through the town, now and again drawing his tattered cloak tighter to shield his body from the cold and biting wind. From some houses standing apart came the sound of grinding mills and the sweet voices of women singing at their work, and these sounds helped him along his lonely way. Except for the occasional bark of a dog, the distant steps of a workman going early to work or the screech of a bird disturbed before its time, the whole town was wrapped in deathly silence. Most of its inhabitants were still in the arms of sleep, a sleep which grew more and more profound on account of the intense winter cold; for the cold used sleep to extend its sway over all things even as a false friend lulls his chosen victim with caressing smiles. The old man, shivering at times but fixed of purpose,[1] plodded on till he came out of the town gate on to a straight road. Along this he now went at a somewhat slower pace, supporting himself on his old staff.

On one side of the road was a row of trees, on the other the town's public garden. The night was darker now and the cold more intense, for the wind was blowing straight along the road and on it there only fell, like frozen snow, the faint light of the morning star. At the end of the garden stood a handsome building of the newest style, and light gleamed through the crevices of its closed doors and windows.

Beholding the wooden arch of this building, the old man was

filled with the joy that the pilgrim feels when he first sees the goal of his journey. On the arch hung an old board with the newly painted letters POST OFFICE. The old man went in quietly and squatted on the veranda. The voices of the two or three people busy at their routine work could be heard faintly through the wall.

"Police Superintendent," a voice inside called sharply. The old man started at the sound, but composed himself again to wait. But for the faith and love that warmed him he could not have borne the bitter cold.

Name after name rang out from within as the clerk read out the English addresses on the letters and flung them to the waiting postmen. From long practice he had acquired great speed in reading out the titles — Commissioner, Superintendent, Diwan Sahib, Librarian — and in flinging out the letters.

In the midst of this procedure a jesting voice from inside called, "Coachman Ali!"

The old man got up, raised his eyes to Heaven in gratitude and, stepping forward, put his hand on the door.

"Godul Bhai!"

"Yes. Who's there?"

"You called out Coachman Ali's name, didn't you? Here I am. I have come for my letter."

"It is a madman, sir, who worries us by calling every day for letters that never come," said the clerk to the postmaster.

The old man went back slowly to the bench on which he had been accustomed to sit for five long years.

Ali had once been a clever shikari.[2] As his skill increased so did his love for the hunt, till at last it was as impossible for him to pass a day without it as it is for the opium eater to forgo his daily portion. When Ali sighted the earth-brown partridge, almost invisible to other eyes, the poor bird, they said, was as good as in his bag. His sharp eyes would see the hare crouching in its form. When even the dogs failed to see the creature cunningly hidden in the yellow-brown scrub, Ali's eagle eyes would catch sight of its ears; and in another moment it was dead. Besides this, he would often go with his friends, the fishermen.

But when the evening of his life was drawing in, he left his old ways and suddenly took a new turn. His only child, Miriam, married and left him. She went off with a soldier to his regiment in the Punjab,[3] and for the last five years he had had no news of this daughter for whose sake alone he dragged on a cheerless existence.

171

Now he understood the meaning of love and separation. He could no longer enjoy the sportsman's pleasure and laugh at the bewildered terror of the young partridges bereft[4] of their parents.

Although the hunter's instinct was in his very blood and bones, such a loneliness had come into his life since the day Miriam had gone away that now, forgetting his sport, he would become lost in admiration of the green cornfields. He reflected deeply and came to the conclusion that the whole universe is built up through love and that the grief of separation is inescapable. And seeing this, he sat down under a tree and wept bitterly. From that day he had risen each morning at four o'clock to walk to the post office. In his whole life he had never received a letter, but with a devout serenity born of hope and faith he continued and was always the first to arrive.

The post office, one of the most uninteresting buildings in the world, became his place of pilgrimage.[5] He always occupied a particular seat in a particular corner of the building, and when people got to know his habit they laughed at him. The postmen began to make a game of him. Even though there was no letter for him, they would call out his name for the fun of seeing him jump and come to the door. But with boundless faith and infinite patience he came every day — and went away empty-handed.

While Ali waited, peons[6] would come for their firms' letters and he would hear them discussing their masters' scandals. These smart young peons in their spotless turbans and creaking shoes were always eager to express themselves. Meanwhile the door would be thrown open and the postmaster, a man with a head as sad and inexpressive as a pumpkin, would be seen sitting on his chair inside. There was no glimmer of animation in his features; and such men usually prove to be village schoolmasters, office clerks, or postmasters.

One day he was there as usual and did not move from his seat when the door was opened.

"Police Commissioner!" the clerk called out, and a young fellow stepped forward briskly for the letters.

"Superintendent!" Another peon came; and so the clerk, like a worshiper of Vishnu,[7] repeated his customary thousand names.

At last they had all gone. Ali too got up and, saluting the post office as though it housed some precious relic, went off, a pitiable figure, a century behind his time.

"That fellow," asked the postmaster, "is he mad?"

"Who, sir? Oh, yes," answered the clerk. "No matter what sort of weather, he has been here every day for the last five years. But he doesn't get many letters."

"I can well understand that! Who does he think will have time to write to him every day?"

"But he's a bit touched, sir. In the old days he committed many sins; and maybe he shed blood within some sacred precincts[8] and is paying for it now," the postman added in support to his statement.

"Madmen are strange people," the postmaster said.

"Yes. Once I saw a madman in Ahmedabad who did absolutely nothing but make little heaps of dust. Another had a habit of going every day to the river in order to pour water on a certain stone!"

"Oh, that's nothing," chimed in another. "I knew one madman who paced up and down all day long, another who never ceased declaiming poetry, and a third who would slap himself on the cheek and then begin to cry out because he was being beaten."

And everyone in the post office began talking of lunacy. All working-class people have a habit of taking periodic rests by joining in general discussion for a few minutes. After listening a little, the postmaster got up and said:

"It seems as though the mad live in a world of their own making. To them, perhaps, we too, appear mad. The madman's world is rather like the poet's, I should think!"

He laughed as he spoke the last words, looking at one of the clerks who wrote indifferent[9] verse. Then he went out and the office became still again.

For several days Ali had not come to the post office. There was no one with enough sympathy or understanding to guess the reason, but all were curious to know what had stopped the old man.

At last he came again; but it was a struggle for him to breathe, and on his face were clear signs of his approaching end. That day he could not contain his impatience.

"Master Sahib," he begged the postmaster, "have you a letter from my Miriam?"

The postmaster was in a hurry to get out to the country.

"What a pest you are, brother!" he exclaimed.

"My name is Ali," answered Ali absentmindedly.

"I know! I know! But do you think we've got your Miriam's name registered?"

"Then please note it down, brother. It will be useful if a letter should come when I am not here." For how should the villager who had spent three quarters of his life hunting know that Miriam's name was not worth a pice[10] to anyone but her father?

The postmaster was beginning to lose his temper. "Have you no sense?" he cried. "Get away! Do you think we are going to eat your letter when it comes?" And he walked off hastily. Ali came out very slowly, turning after every few steps to gaze at the post office. His eyes were filling with tears of helplessness, for his patience was exhausted, even though he still had faith. Yet how could he still hope to hear from Miriam?

Ali heard one of the clerks coming up behind him and turned to him.

"Brother!" he said.

The clerk was surprised, but being a decent fellow he said, "Well?"

"Here, look at this!" and Ali produced an old tin box and emptied five golden guineas[11] into the surprised clerk's hands. "Do not look so startled," he continued. "They will be useful to you, and they can never be so to me. But will you do one thing?"

"What?"

"What do you see up there?" said Ali, pointing to the sky.

"Heaven."

"Allah[12] is there, and in His presence I am giving you this money. When it comes, you must forward my Miriam's letter to me."

"But where — where am I to send it?" asked the utterly bewildered clerk.

"To my grave."

"What?"

"Yes. It is true. Today is my last day: my very last, alas! And I have not seen Miriam, I have had no letter from her." Tears were in Ali's eyes as the clerk slowly left him and went on his way with the five golden guineas in his pocket.

Ali was never seen again and no one troubled to inquire after him.

One day, however, trouble came to the postmaster. His daughter lay ill in another town and he was anxiously waiting for news from her. The post was brought in and the letters piled on the table. Seeing an envelope of the color and shape he expected, the postmaster eagerly snatched it up. It was addressed to coachman Ali, and he dropped it as though it had given him an electric shock. The haughty temper of the official had quite left him in his sorrow and anxiety and had laid bare his human heart. He knew at once that this was the letter the old man had been waiting for: it must be from his daughter Miriam.

"Lakshmi Das!" called the postmaster, for such was the name of the clerk to whom Ali had given his money.

"Yes, sir?"

"This is for your old coachman Ali. Where is he now?"

"I will find out, sir."

The postmaster did not receive his own letter all that day.

He worried all night and, getting up at three, went to sit in the office. "When Ali comes at four o'clock," he mused, "I will give him the letter myself."

For now the postmaster understood all Ali's heart, and his very soul. After spending but a single night in suspense, anxiously waiting for news of his daughter, his heart was brimming with sympathy for the poor old man who had spent his nights for the last five years in the same suspense. At the stroke of five he heard a soft knock on the door: he felt sure it was Ali. He rose quickly from his chair, his suffering father's heart recognizing another, and flung the door wide open.

"Come in, brother Ali," he cried, handing the letter to the meek old man, bent double with age, who was standing outside. Ali was leaning on a stick and the tears were wet on his face as they had been when the clerk left him. But his features had been hard then and now they were softened by lines of kindliness. He lifted his

175

eyes and in them was a light so unearthly that the postmaster shrank in fear and astonishment.

Lakshmi Das had heard the postmaster's words as he came towards the office from another quarter. "Who was that, sir? Old Ali?" he asked. But the postmaster took no notice of him. He was staring with wide-open eyes at the doorway from which Ali had disappeared. Where could he have gone? At last he turned to Lakshmi Das. "Yes, I was speaking to Ali," he said.

"Old Ali is dead, sir. But give me his letter."

"What! But when? Are you sure, Lakshmi Das?"

"Yes, it is so," broke in a postman who had just arrived. "Ali died three months ago."

The postmaster was bewildered. Miriam's letter was still lying near the door; Ali's image was still before his eyes. He listened to Lakshmi Das's recital of the last interview, but he could still not doubt the reality of the knock on the door and the tears in Ali's eyes. He was perplexed. Had he really seen Ali? Had his imagination deceived him? Or had it perhaps been Lakshmi Das?

The daily routine began. The clerk read out the addresses — Police Commissioner, Superintendent, Librarian — and flung the letters deftly.

But the postmaster now watched them as though each contained a warm, beating heart. He no longer thought of them in terms of envelopes and postcards. He saw the essential, human worth of a letter.

That evening you might have seen Lakshmi Das and the postmaster walking with slow steps to Ali's grave. They laid the letter on it and turned back.

"Lakshmi Das, were you indeed the first to come to the office this morning?"

"Yes, sir, I was the first."

"Then how . . . No, I don't understand. . . ."

"What, sir?"

"Oh, never mind," the postmaster said shortly. At the office he parted from Lakshmi Das and went in. The newly-waked father's heart in him was reproaching[13] him for having failed to understand Ali's anxiety. Tortured by doubt and remorse, he sat down in the glow of the charcoal sigri[14] to wait.

1 **fixed of purpose:** determined
2 **shikari:** hunter
3 **Punjab:** a state in India
4 **bereft:** deprived of something cherished, especially by death
5 **pilgrimage:** long journey to some sacred place
6 **peons:** workers who perform tasks for their employers
7 **Vishnu:** one of the three chief Hindu gods. Vishnu is the preserver and the protector of the world.
8 **precincts:** the grounds immediately surrounding a temple or other sacred building
9 **indifferent:** mediocre; neither good nor bad
10 **pice:** Indian currency
11 **guineas:** former British gold coins (used in India)
12 **Allah:** the Moslem name for God
13 **reproaching:** blaming
14 **sigri:** hearth

# A CLOSER LOOK

*1. How does Ali come to understand the meaning of "love and separation"? Explain why the post office becomes his "place of pilgrimage." Why does he keep going to the post office instead of giving up? Why do the postal workers make fun of him?*

*2. Why does Ali give the postal clerk five golden guineas? Where does he want the clerk to forward Miriam's letter? Why?*

*3. What is the "trouble" that comes to the postmaster? Why does he finally understand how Ali felt during the long period of time he waited for Miriam's letter?*

*4. The postmaster is worrying about his own daughter when the letter from Miriam finally comes. That same night, he goes to his office to wait for Ali. Do you think he really sees Ali that night, does he see Ali's ghost, or does he see a figment of his own imagination? Explain your answer.*

*5. After the "visit" from Ali, the postmaster no longer sees letters in terms of envelopes and postcards. How does he see them? Why does he go with his clerk to place Miriam's letter on Ali's grave? Why does he reproach himself for having failed to understand Ali's anxiety?*

● If something bad were to happen to you, would you rather have it come as a result of your own actions, or as a result of something beyond your control (an accident, for example)? Mary Lavin gives us reason to think about that question in "The Story of the Widow's Son." It is a story that takes place in Ireland. And it is a story that has two endings.

## Mary Lavin

# THE STORY OF THE WIDOW'S SON

THERE WAS ONCE A WIDOW, LIVING IN A SMALL neglected village at the foot of a steep hill. She had only one son, but he was the meaning of her life. She lived for his sake. She wore herself out working for him. Every day she made a hundred sacrifices in order to keep him at a good school in the town, four miles away, because there was a better teacher than the village dullard that had taught herself.

She made great plans for Packy, but she did not tell him about her plans. Instead she threatened him, day and night, that if he didn't turn out well, she would put him to work on the roads, or in the quarry under the hill.

But as the years went by, everyone in the village, and even Packy himself, could tell by the way she watched him out of sight in the morning, and watched to see him come into sight in the evening, that he was the beat of her heart, and that her gruff words were only a cover for her pride and joy in him.

It was for Packy's sake that she walked for hours along the road, letting her cow graze the long acre of the wayside grass, in order to spare the few poor blades that pushed up through the stones in her own field. It was for his sake she walked back and forth to the town to sell a few cabbages as soon as ever they were fit. It was for his sake that she got up in the cold dawning hours to gather mushrooms that would take the place of foods that had to be bought with money. She bent her back daily to make every penny she could, and, as often happens, she made more by industry, out of her few bald acres, than many of the farmers around her made out of their great bearded meadows. Out of the money she made by selling eggs alone, she paid for Packy's clothes and for the greater number of his books.

When Packy was fourteen, he was in the last class in the school, and the master had great hopes of his winning a scholarship to a big college in the city. He was getting to be a tall lad, and his features were beginning to take a strong cast.[1] His character was strengthening, too, under his mother's sharp tongue. The people of the village were beginning to give him the same respect they gave to the sons of the farmers who came from their fine colleges in the summer, with blue suits and bright ties. And whenever they spoke to the widow they praised him up to the skies.

One day in June the widow was waiting at the gate for Packy. There had been no rain for some days and the hens and chickens were pecking irritably at the dry ground and wandering up and down the road in bewilderment. A neighbor passed.

"Waiting for Packy?" said the neighbor, pleasantly, and he stood for a minute to take off his hat and wipe the sweat of the day from his face. He was an old man.

"It's a hot day!" he said. "It will be a hard push for Packy on that battered old bike of his. I wouldn't like to have to face into four miles on a day like this!"

"Packy would travel three times that distance if there was a book at the other end of the road!" said the widow, with the pride of those who cannot read more than a line or two without wearying.

The minutes went by slowly. The widow kept looking up at the sun.

"I suppose the heat is better than the rain!" she said, at last.

"The heat can do a lot of harm too, though," said the neighbor, absentmindedly, as he pulled a long blade of grass from between the stones of the wall and began to chew the end of it. "You could get sunstroke on a day like this!" He looked up at the sun. "The sun is a terror," he said. "It could cause you to drop down dead like a stone!"

The widow strained out further over the gate. She looked up the hill in the direction of the town.

"He will have a good cool breeze coming down the hill, at any rate," she said.

The man looked up the hill.

"That's true. On the hottest day of the year you would get a cool breeze coming down that hill on a bicycle. You would feel the air streaming past your cheeks like silk. And in the winter it's like two knives flashing to either side of you, and peeling off your skin like you'd peel the bark off a sally-rod." He chewed the grass meditatively. "That hill is a hill worthy of the name of a hill." He took the grass out of his mouth. "It's my belief," he said earnestly, looking at the widow, "it's my belief that that hill is to be found marked with a name in the Ordnance Survey map!"

"If that's the case," said the widow, "Packy will be able to tell you all about it. When it isn't a book he has in his hand it's a map."

"Is that so?" said the man. "That's interesting. A map is a great thing. It isn't everyone can make out a map."

The widow wasn't listening.

"I think I see Packy!" she said, and she opened the wooden gate and stepped out into the roadway.

At the top of the hill there was a glitter of spokes as a bicycle came into sight. Then there was a flash of blue jersey as Packy came flying downward, gripping the handle bars of the bike, with his bright hair blown back from his forehead. The hill was so steep, and he came down so fast, that it seemed to the man and woman at the bottom of the hill that he was not moving at all, but that it was the bright trees and bushes, the bright ditches and wayside grasses, that were streaming away to either side of him.

The hens and chickens clucked and squawked and ran along the

road looking for a safe place in the ditches. They ran to either side with feminine fuss and chatter. Packy waved to his mother. He came nearer and nearer. They could see the freckles on his face.

"Shoo!" said Packy's mother, lifting her apron and flapping it in the air to frighten them out of his way.

It was only afterwards, when the harm was done, that the widow began to think that it might, perhaps, have been the flapping of her own apron that frightened the old clucking hen, and sent her flying out over the garden wall into the middle of the road.

The old hen appeared suddenly on top of the grassy ditch and looked with a distraught eye at the hens and chickens as they ran to right and left. Her own feathers began to stand out from her. She craned her neck forward and gave a distracted squawk, and fluttered down into the middle of the hot dusty road.

Packy jammed on the brakes. The widow screamed. There was a flurry of white feathers and a spurt of blood. The bicycle swerved and fell. Packy was thrown over the handlebars.

It was such a simple accident that, although the widow screamed, and although the old man looked around to see if there was help near, neither of them thought that Packy was very badly hurt, but when they ran over and lifted his head, and saw that he could not speak, they wiped the blood from his face and looked around, desperately, to measure the distance they would have to carry him.

It was only a few yards to the door of the cottage, but Packy was

dead before they got him across the threshold.

"He's only in a weakness!" screamed the widow, and she urged the crowd that gathered outside the door to do something for him. "Get a doctor!" she cried, pushing a young laborer toward the door. "Hurry! Hurry! The doctor will bring him around."

But the neighbors that kept coming in the door, quickly, from all sides, were crossing themselves, one after another, and falling on their knees, as soon as they laid eyes on the boy, stretched out flat on the bed, with the dust and dirt and the sweat marks of life on his dead face.

When at last the widow was convinced that her son was dead, the other women had to hold her down. She waved her arms and wrestled to get free. She wanted to wring the neck of every hen in the yard.

"I'll kill every one of them. What good are they to me, now? All the hens in the world aren't worth one drop of human blood. That old clucking hen wasn't worth more than six shillings,[2] at the very most. What is six shillings? Is it worth poor Packy's life?"

But after a time she stopped raving and looked from one face to another.

"Why didn't he ride over the old hen?" she asked. "Why did he try to save an old hen that wasn't worth more than six shillings? Didn't he know he was worth more to his mother than an old hen that would be going into the pot one of these days? Why did he do it? Why did he put on the brakes going down one of the worst hills in the country? Why? Why?"

The neighbors patted her arm.

"There now!" they said. "There now!" And that was all they could think of saying, and they said it over and over again. "There now! There now!"

And years afterwards, whenever the widow spoke of her son Packy to the neighbors who dropped in to keep her company for an hour or two, she always had the same question.

"Why did he put the price of an old clucking hen above the price of his own life?"

And the people always gave her the same answer. "There now!" they said. "There now!" And they sat as silently as the widow herself, looking into the fire.

But surely some of those neighbors must have been stirred to wonder what would have happened had Packy not yielded to his impulse of fear, and had, instead, ridden boldly over the old clucking hen? And surely some of them must have stared into the flames and pictured the scene of the accident again, altering a detail here and there as they did so, and giving the story a different end. For these people knew the widow, and they knew Packy, and when you know people well it is as easy to guess what they would say and do in certain circumstances as it is to remember what they actually did say and do in other circumstances. In fact it is sometimes easier to invent than to remember accurately, and were this not so, two great branches of creative art would wither in an hour: the art of the storyteller and the art of the gossip. So, perhaps, if I try to tell you what I myself think might have happened had Packy killed that cackling old hen, you will not accuse me of abusing my privileges as a writer. After all, what I am about to tell you is no more of a fiction than what I have already told, and I lean no heavier now upon your credulity[3] than, with your full consent, I did in the first instance.

And moreover, in many respects the new story is the same as the old.

It begins in the same way too. There is the widow grazing her cow by the wayside, and walking the long roads to the town, weighted down with sacks of cabbages that will pay for Packy's schooling. There she is, fussing over Packy in the mornings in case he would be late for school. There she is in the evening watching the battered clock on the dresser for the hour when he will appear on the top of the hill at his return. And there too, on a hot day in June, is the old laboring man coming up the road, and pausing to talk to her as she stands at the door. There he is dragging a blade of grass from between the stones of the wall and putting it between his teeth to chew, before he opens his mouth.

And when he opens his mouth at last it is to utter the same remark.

"Waiting for Packy?" said the old man, and then he took off his hat and wiped the sweat from his forehead. It will be remembered that he was an old man. "It's a hot day," he said.

"It's very hot," said the widow, looking anxiously up the hill. "It's a hot day to push a bicycle four miles along a bad road with the dust rising to choke you, and the sun striking spikes off the handle bars!"

"The heat is better than the rain, all the same," said the old man.

"I suppose it is," said the widow. "There were days when Packy

183

came home with the rain dried into his clothes so bad they stood up stiff like boards when he took them off. They stood up stiff like boards against the wall, for all the world as if he was still standing in them!"

"Is that so?" said the old man. "You may be sure he got a good petting on those days. There is no son like a widow's son. A ewe lamb!"

"Is it Packy?" said the widow, in disgust. "Packy never got a day's petting since the day he was born. I made up my mind from the first that I'd never make a soft one out of him."

The widow looked up the hill again, and set herself to raking the gravel outside the gate as if she were in the road for no other purpose. Then she gave another look up the hill.

"Here he is now!" she said, and she raised such a cloud of dust with the rake that they could hardly see the glitter of the bicycle spokes and the flash of blue jersey as Packy came down the hill at a breakneck speed.

Nearer and nearer he came, faster and faster, waving his hand to the widow, shouting at the hens to leave the way!

The hens ran for the ditches, stretching their necks in gawky terror. And then, as the last hen squawked into the ditch, the way was clear for a moment before the whirling silver spokes.

Then, unexpectedly, up from nowhere it seemed, came an old clucking hen and, clucking despairingly, it stood for a moment on

the top of the wall and then rose into the air with the clumsy flight of a ground fowl.

Packy stopped whistling. The widow screamed. Packy yelled and the widow flapped her apron. Then Packy swerved the bicycle, and a cloud of dust rose from the braked wheel.

For a minute it could not be seen what exactly had happened, but Packy put his foot down and dragged it along the ground in the dust till he brought the bicycle to a sharp stop. He threw the bicycle down with a clatter on the hard road and ran back. The widow could not bear to look. She threw her apron over her head.

"He's killed the clucking hen!" she said. "He's killed her! He's killed her!" and then she let the apron fall back into place, and began to run up the hill herself. The old man spat out the blade of grass that he had been chewing and ran after the woman.

"Did you kill it?" screamed the widow, and as she got near enough to see the blood and feathers, she raised her arm over her head, and her fist was clenched till the knuckles shone white. Packy cowered down over the carcass of the fowl and hunched up his shoulders as if to shield himself from a blow. His legs were spattered with blood, and the brown and white feathers of the dead hen were stuck to his hands, and stuck to his clothes, as they were strewn[4] all over the road. Some of the short white inner feathers were still swirling with the dust in the air.

"I couldn't help it, Mother. I couldn't help it. I didn't see her till it was too late!"

The widow caught up the hen and examined it all over, holding it by the bone of the breast, and letting the long neck dangle. Then, catching it by the leg, she raised it suddenly above her head, and brought down the bleeding body on the boy's back, in blow after blow, spattering the blood all over his face and his hands, over his clothes and over the white dust of the road around him.

"How dare you lie to me!" she screamed, gaspingly, between the blows. "You saw the hen, I know you saw it. You stopped whistling! You called out! We were watching you. We saw." She turned upon the old man. "Isn't that right?" she demanded. "He saw the hen, didn't he? He saw it?"

"It looked that way," said the old man, uncertainly, his eye on the dangling fowl in the widow's hand.

"There you are!" said the widow. She threw the hen down on the road. "You saw the hen in front of you on the road, as plain as you see it now," she accused, "but you wouldn't stop to save it

because you were in too big a hurry to get home to fill your belly!
Isn't that so?"

"No, Mother. No! I saw her all right but it was too late to do
anything."

"He admits now that he saw it," said the widow, turning and
nodding triumphantly at the onlookers who had gathered at the
sound of the shouting.

"I never denied seeing it!" said the boy, appealing to the
onlookers as to his judges.

"He doesn't deny it!" screamed the widow. "He stands there
brazen as you like, and admits for all the world to hear that he saw
the hen as plain as the nose on his face, and he rode over it without
a thought!"

"But what else could I do?" said the boy, throwing out his hand,
appealing to the crowd now, and now appealing to the widow. "If
I'd put on the brakes going down the hill at such a speed I would
have been put over the handle bars!"

"And what harm would that have done you?" screamed the
widow. "I often saw you taking a toss when you were wrestling
with Jimmy Mack and I heard no complaints afterwards, although
your elbows and knees would be running blood, and your face
scraped like a gridiron!"[5] She turned to the crowd. "That's as true
as God. I often saw him come in with his nose spouting blood like
a pump, and one eye closed as tight as the eye of a corpse. My hand
was often stiff for a week from sopping out wet cloths to put
poultices[6] on him and try to bring his face back to rights again."
She swung back to Packy again. "You're not afraid of a fall when
you go climbing trees, are you? You're not afraid to go up on the
roof after a cat, are you? Oh, there's more in this than you want me
to know. I can see that. You killed that hen on purpose — that's
what I believe! You're tired of going to school. You want to get out
of going away to college. That's it! You think if you kill the few
poor hens we have there will be no money in the box when the time
comes to pay for books and classes. That's it!" Packy began to
redden.

"It's late in the day for me to be thinking of things like that," he
said. "It's long ago I should have started those tricks if that was
the way I felt. But it's not true. I want to go to college. The reason I
was coming down the hill so fast was to tell you that I got the
scholarship. The teacher told me as I was leaving the schoolhouse.
That's why I was pedaling so hard. That's why I was whistling.

186

That's why I was waving my hand. Didn't you see me waving my hand from once I came in sight at the top of the hill?"

The widow's hands fell to her sides. The wind of words died down within her and left her flat and limp. She didn't know what to say. She could feel the neighbors staring at her. She wished that they were gone away about their business. She wanted to throw out her arms to the boy to drag him against her heart and hug him like a small child. But she thought of how the crowd would look at each other and nod and snigger. A ewe lamb! She didn't want to satisfy them. If she gave in to her feelings now they would know how much she had been counting on his getting the scholarship. She wouldn't please them! She wouldn't satisfy them!

She looked at Packy, and when she saw him standing there before her, spattered with the furious feathers and crude blood of the dead hen, she felt a fierce disappointment for the boy's own disappointment, and a fierce resentment against him for killing the hen on this day of all days, and spoiling the great news of his success.

Her mind was in confusion. She stared at the blood on his face, and all at once it seemed as if the blood was a bad omen of the future that was for him. Disappointment, fear, resentment, and above all defiance, raised themselves within her like screeching animals. She looked from Packy to the onlookers.

"Scholarship! Scholarship!" she sneered, putting as much derision as she could into her voice and expression.

"I suppose you think you are a great fellow now? I suppose you think you are independent now? I suppose you think you can go off with yourself now, and look down on your poor slave of a mother who scraped and sweated for you with her cabbages and her hens? I suppose you think to yourself that it doesn't matter now whether the hens are alive or dead? Is that the way? Well, let me tell you this! You're not as independent as you think. The scholarship may pay for your books and teachers' fees but who will pay for your clothes? Ah-ha, you forgot that, didn't you?" She put her hands on her hips.

Packy hung his head. He no longer appealed to the gawking neighbors. They might have been able to save him from blows, but he knew enough about life to know that no one could save him from shame.

The widow's heart burned at the sight of his shamed face, as her heart burned with grief, but her temper too burned fiercer and fiercer, and she came to a point at which nothing could quell the blaze till it had burned itself out. "Who'll buy your suits?" she yelled. "Who'll buy your boots?" She paused to think of more humiliating accusations. "Who'll buy your breeches?" She paused again and her teeth bit against each other. What would wound deepest? What shame could she drag upon him? "Who'll buy your nightshirts or will you sleep in your skin?"

The neighbors laughed at that and the tension was broken. The widow herself laughed. She held her sides and laughed, and as she laughed everything seemed to take on a newer and simpler significance. Things were not as bad as they seemed a moment before. She wanted Packy to laugh, too. She looked at him. But as she looked at Packy her heart turned cold with a strange new fear.

"Get into the house!" she said, giving him a push ahead of her. She wanted him safe under her own roof. She wanted to get him away from the gaping neighbors. She hated them, man, woman, and child. She felt that if they had not been there things would have been different. And she wanted to get away from the sight of the blood on the road. She wanted to mash a few potatoes and make a bit of potato cake for Packy. That would comfort him. He loved that.

Packy hardly touched the food. And even after he had washed and scrubbed himself there were stains of blood turning up in unexpected places: behind his ears, under his fingernails, inside the cuff of his sleeve.

"Put on your good clothes," said the widow, making a great effort to be gentle, but her manner had become as twisted and as hard as the branches of the trees across the road from her, and even the kindly offers she made sounded harsh. The boy sat on the chair in a slumped position that kept her nerves on edge and set up a further conflict of irritation and love in her heart. She hated to see him slumping in the chair, not asking to go outside the door, but still she was uneasy whenever he as much as looked in the direction of the door. She felt safe while he was under the roof; inside the lintel;[7] under her eyes.

Next day she went in to wake him for school, but his room was empty; his bed had not been slept in, and when she ran out into the yard and called him everywhere, there was no answer. She ran up and down. She called at the houses of the neighbors but he was not in any house. And she thought she could hear sniggering behind her in each house that she left, as she ran to another one. He wasn't

188

in the village. He wasn't in the town. The master of the school said that she should let the police have a description of him. He said he had never met a boy as sensitive as Packy. A boy like that took strange notions into his head from time to time.

The police did their best but there was no news of Packy that night. A few days later there was a letter saying that he was well. He asked his mother to notify the master that he would not be coming back, so that some other boy could claim the scholarship. He said that he would send the price of the hen as soon as he made some money.

Another letter in a few weeks said that he had got a job on a trawler,[8] and that he would not be able to write very often but that he would put aside some of his pay every week and send it to his mother whenever he got into port. He said that he wanted to pay her back for all she had done for him. He gave no address. He kept his promise about the money but he never gave any address when he wrote.

And so the people may have let their thoughts run on, as they sat by the fire with the widow, listening to her complaining voice saying the same thing over and over. "Why did he put the price of

an old hen above the price of his own life?" And it is possible that their version of the story has a certain element of truth about it too. Perhaps all our actions have this double quality about them, this possibility of alternative; and that it is only by careful watching and absolute sincerity that we follow the path that is destined[9] for us, and no matter how tragic that may be, it is better than the tragedy we bring upon ourselves.

[1] **cast:** form; appearance
[2] **shillings:** former British currency (used in Ireland)
[3] **credulity:** willingness to believe
[4] **strewn:** scattered
[5] **gridiron:** a grate for broiling food
[6] **poultice:** soft, warm, usually medicated mass spread on cloth and applied to sores or other wounds
[7] **lintel:** a horizontal beam over the top of a door or window
[8] **trawler:** a type of fishing boat
[9] **destined:** caused by fate

## A CLOSER LOOK

*1. At the end of the story, the author says, "Perhaps all our actions have this double quality about them, this possibility of alternative. . . ." What alternatives did Packy have when the hen ran in front of his speeding bike? Which alternative did he choose in the first version of the story? Which did he choose in the second version? What alternatives did the widow have when Packy killed the hen? Which did she choose?*

*2. After reading both versions of the story, we can conclude that Packy is a sensitive boy with a strong sense of duty and gratitude toward his mother for the sacrifices she has made for him. We can also conclude that though the widow loves her son, she is a domineering mother who is determined to make Packy fit her image of successful manhood at any cost. Based on what we know about both characters, explain why Packy decided to risk injury rather than kill the hen in the first version of the story. In the second version, why did the widow continue to scold Packy after he told her he had won the scholarship?*

*3. In both versions of the story, the widow hides her true feelings of love for her son. Find examples, in both versions, of her insincerity.*

*4. Explain why the second ending of the story is harder for the widow to bear than the first.*

**ACKNOWLEDGMENTS** *(continued from page 2)*

**The Curtis Publishing Company** for "A Wild Goose Falls" by Edmund Gilligan. Reprinted from *The Saturday Evening Post*. Copyright © 1961 The Curtis Publishing Company.

**Delacorte Press** for "Harrison Bergeron" from WELCOME TO THE MONKEY HOUSE by Kurt Vonnegut, Jr. Copyright © 1961 by Kurt Vonnegut, Jr. Originally published in *Fantasy and Science Fiction* Magazine. Reprinted by permission of Delacorte Press/ Seymour Lawrence, a division of BANTAM, DOUBLEDAY, DELL PUBLISHING GROUP, INC.

**Devin-Adair Company** for "The Story of the Widow's Son" by Mary Lavin from 44 IRISH SHORT STORIES, edited by Devin A. Garrity. Copyright © 1955 by The Devin-Adair Company, and reprinted by their permission.

**Frederick Fell Publishers, Inc.** for "A Favor for Lefty" by Charles Einstein from ANTHOLOGY OF BEST SHORT-SHORT STORIES, Volume 7, edited by Robert Oberfirst. Copyright © 1959 by Thomas Oberfirst. Reprinted by permission of the publisher.

**Angel Flores** for "A Letter to God" by Gregorio Lopez y Fuentes, from GREAT SPANISH SHORT STORIES, edited by Angel Flores. New York, Dell, 1962. Copyright © 1962 by Angel Flores. Reprinted by permission of Angel Flores.

**Harcourt Brace Jovanovich, Inc.,** for "Everyday Use" by Alice Walker from IN LOVE AND TROUBLE: STORIES OF BLACK WOMEN. Copyright © 1973 by Alice Walker. Reprinted by permission of Harcourt Brace Jovanovich, Inc.

**Lin Hsiang Ju** for "The Tiger" by Li Fu-yen from FAMOUS CHINESE SHORT STORIES retold by Lin Yutang. Copyright 1948, 1951, 1952, by Lin Yutang. Reprinted by permission of Lin Yutang.

**Alan Marshall** for "The Dog," from FOUR SUNDAY SUITS AND OTHER STORIES by Alan Marshall. Copyright © 1973, 1975 by Alan Marshall.

**Harold Matson Company, Inc.** for "Thus I Refute Beelzy" by John Collier. Copyright © 1940 by John Collier, copyright renewed 1967. Reprinted by permission of Harold Matson Company, Inc.

**Oxford University Press** for "The Letter," by Gaurishanker Joshi. Reprinted from TEN TALES FOR INDIAN STUDENTS by permission of the Oxford University Press.

**Random House, Inc.** for "A Christmas Memory," by Truman Capote. Copyright © 1956 by Truman Capote. Reprinted from SELECTED WRITINGS OF TRUMAN CAPOTE by permission of Random House, Inc.

**Scholastic Inc.** for "The Carnival" by Michael Fedo. Copyright © 1968 by Scholastic Magazines, Inc. Reprinted by permission of the publisher.

**Charles Scribner's Sons, an imprint of Macmillan Publishing Company,** for "The Far and the Near" by Thomas Wolfe from FROM DEATH TO MORNING by Thomas Wolfe. Copyright 1935 by Charles Scribner's Sons; renewal copyright © 1963 by Paul Gitlin. Reprinted with permission of Charles Scribner's Sons, an imprint of Macmillan Publishing Company.

**ILLUSTRATION AND PHOTOGRAPHY CREDITS**

Andrea Baruffi, *pages 4-5, 6, 64, 122.* Greg Rudd, *pages 9, 34, 36, 67, 69, 71.* Ron Sauber, *pages 22, 25, 29, 57, 59, 63, 180–181, 184, 189.* Jack Williams, *pages 40, 42, 131, 135.* Courtesy of the New York Public Library Picture Collection, *pages 51, 52* (Quilt made by Amanda and Anna Yoder, 1930). Maria Horvath, *pages 79, 81.* Dick Bangham, *pages 99, 103, 116, 118-119, 120.* Bobbi Tull, *pages 126, 128.* Courtesy of ABC TV "Studio 67," *pages 139, 149.* Courtesy of Ringling Brothers Barnum & Bailey Circus, *pages 152-153.* Susan Borduin, *pages 162, 168.*